THE EARLY YEARS

JACK FROST XI

1961-1999

Tossing for Innings
Author, Tony Gill tosses for innings on the Carvers, Ringwood, Hampshire, Jack Frost XI v The Citroen XI. 18th June, 1968.
Left to Right: W.A.Smith and R.Harman (Surrey), P.B.H.May, CBE (Surrey and England), Lionel Citroen, J.H.Edrich, MBE (Surrey and England) Sir Alec V Bedser (Surrey and England), Tony Gill, E.A.Bedser (Surrey)

THE EARLY YEARS
JACK FROST XI
1961-1999

Tony Gill

*To Roger Dennett.
You're doing a good job.
Best regards
Tony Gill*

First published in Great Britain 2000
by Bards Original Publishing
Studio 1, 9 The Mount, Burtons' St. Leonards,
East Sussex TN38 0HR, United Kingdom
Telephone/Facsimile: 01424 201 029
e-mail: bards.original@ukgateway.net

© Tony Gill 2000

All rights reserved. No part of this publication may be reproduced or transmitted in any form or by any means, electronic or mechanical including photocopying, recording or any information storage or retrieval system, without prior permission in writing from the publishers.

The right of Tony Gill to be identified as author of this work has been asserted by him in accordance with the Copyright, Designs and Patents Act, 1988

A catalogue record of this book is available from the British Library

ISBN 0 9538975 0 8

Designed and typeset in Great Britain
by Vivitext Graphic Design, 01485 534566
and printed in Great Britain by
Purely Print 01258 459977

*For Harry, Emma and Charlie Firman
and the Spirit of my father
John Gill who first introduced me to
the game with the beautiful name.*

CONTENTS

Prologue		vii
Foreword by K.I.Morell, Esq. OBE		1
Chapter I	Foundation and Early Days	3
Chapter II	First Tours and Onward	9
Chapter III	Mid-Winter Frosting	21
Chapter IV	Home Games	27
Chapter V	Early Sunday Fixture	31
Chapter VI	California Here we Come	35
Chapter VII	1975 and Onward	45
Chapter VIII	Functions of Fun	51
Chapter IX	Gnomes and other Little People	53
Chapter X	To the Present	55
Chapter XI	What's it all about	59
Appendix I	Requiem To A Young Hare	61
Appendix II	Earlier History	63

Acknowledgements

I am indebted to the following for their particular contribution
in making this publication possible.

K.I. Morell, OBE. David Lipop and Vivien J McDonald for their valuable
cooperation in the production of this book.

Special thanks to Liz Wright for her kind permission to use her painting of
JackFrost XI v Leverets at Hare Lane Green, Claygate, on the front cover.

All present and past members of Jack Frost XI,
without whom there would be no history.

PROLOGUE

Welcome to my modest record of the cricket club I was delighted and proud to found in the early nineteen-sixties.

Now at the beginning of the new millennium I have written down all I can recollect of the past forty years.

I would ask readers to bear with me should they find fault in the details because this history is purely from memory, my having no written records of the events whatsoever.

I have titled the work JACK FROST XI – THE EARLY YEARS in the belief and hope that this unique wandering cricket club will prosper for ever.

Tony Gill
President and Founder Jack Frost XI
March 2000

FOREWORD

by K.I.MORELL O.B.E. Chairman of Jack Frost XI for the first 25 years.

Over a few drinks in the Swan after a Leveret/Old Citizen match in September 1961, Tony saw a newspaper seller (Yes! they did print Evening Papers on Saturdays) and decided to buy one. Much to every one's annoyance, we had great difficulty in finding the Cricket Scores among all the Football blurb. This started a discussion about football cutting into OUR SEASON and why did we not fight back. The outcome was a decision that Tony would invite two or three players who regularly played against the Leverets to form a team to play the Leverets on their matting on the Green.

This happened on Boxing Day, we made up our own rules – 20 overs each – Soup and Baked Potatoes for lunch in between. After each 10 overs the batting side sent out a bottle of Scotch with glasses (not forgetting the Umpires).

The whole day was declared a great success largely due to Tony's organisation, so we decided to repeat the exercise the following year, thus we adopted the name JACK FROST.

From these humble beginnings the strong healthy Club as we know it today has grown. Our earliest tour was to the New Forest and this was followed by Roger Hunt's tours to Worcestershire.

In 1975 we played a match in every month of the year including our most ambitious tour to California.

The real health of the Club has been the strength of new members coming through with some of them carrying forward the real spirit of Frost into the future.

KIM

2

Chapter I – FOUNDATION AND EARLY YEARS

The time has come that I should enshrine in stone the circumstances that brought about the foundation of one of the great fun loving wandering cricket clubs of the twentieth century. This does not compare with the origin of the species, the birth of a nation nor the creation of the world, but here I go with the start of what has now become the story of Jack Frost XI.

Having called it a day with the Army, or it may have been the other way round as I had become wary of firing Lee Enfield 303's. Chaps were apt to fire back with Kalashnikovs. I married my young sweetheart, Linda, and set up home in a cottage on the edge of Littleworth Common, in Esher, Surrey. It well suited me to join a nearby cricket club, the **Leverets**, who played, within bag carrying distance, on a matting wicket outside a most convivial hostelry, The Swan at Claygate. The club was named Leverets, as the postage size ground lay between the River Rythe and Hare Lane. Founded at the turn of the last century, and revived by Jimmy O'Connor and others after Hitler's War.

It was named after the "Young Hares" that made up their team. Nevertheless when I joined the total age of the three slips, non-runners and non-benders, totalled over 180 years. Each and every year the Leverets closed their season, on the first Sunday in October, with a match against a local pub, The White Lion, The Winning Horse or The Royal Albert. Towards the very end of the 1961 season it became apparent that none of these local pubs could raise a side. Facing a long dark winter ahead, rather than miss even one fixture, I volunteered to bring a social team against the Leverets to end the season. I then set about gathering together many cricketing friends some of whom had, during the course of that season, played against the **Leveret Cricket Club**. From **Esher C.C.** came Kit Briggs, Tony Hewett, John Halliwell, and Tony Denning keeping wicket. Tony Judd from **Southgate, Old Citizens** provided Alderman K.I. Morell (Croucher) and the distinguished H. Sydney Smith. A delightful left arm bowler from **Norwood**, one J. Alan Hawtin, Keith Ives from **Economicals** and 12th Man Tony Shrimpton from **Ditton Hill**, together with Gilbert Weatherall from **Ashstead**, assembled under my captaincy.

Up to that time my leadership, had not been marked with success. In 1956, for a season I had skippered the regimental cricket team. Despite prevailing on one Brian.G.C. Huggett (The Baron), who later captained the British Ryder Cup Team, to play cricket in return for my making up the team to play in the Army Golf Cup, I failed to record a victory. Mind you my storming of the Suez Canal Zone did disrupt my cricket strategy. Frost managed to accumulate some hundred plus runs before two elevenths of the Leveret's batted, in the shape of veteran Len Coops and young schoolmaster Roger Hunt.

I – FOUNDATION AND EARLY YEARS

Our top rating seam attack having failed to dislodge the Leveret openers, and I, always a believer in left-arm spinners, soon introduced Alan Hawtin into the attack. After five of his first six deliveries were dismissed to the short boundary, Alan commented 'I don't usually bowl that badly'. It was true but not on that sunny October day. Suffice is to say that in the Frost inaugural game we failed to take a wicket.

The Rythe Trophy, named after the geographical designation of the stream marking one boundary, was duly engraved and presented to the home side. (Whatever happened to the Silver Rythe Trophy?) This one-off game of cricket with a pick-up side held on an autumn day was the start of it all. However, much rejoicing in The Swan at having played cricket 'out of season' set the tone for the future of the XI. In the course of time Frost played thirty games against the Leverets. (See Appendix I)

THE TITLE - JACK FROST XI

The name "Jack Frost XI" may be a puzzle to some. It came to mind that, as a cricketer in my twenties, it would be somewhat pompous to call the side H.C.A.Gill's XI. after all I was not a Leveson-Gower, Hon. Ivo. Bligh or Dr. W. G. Grace. I reasoned that as we played in the Autumn and frost may occur at any time, that name would be appropriate. It was always an aim to extend the cricket season in response to Association Football players who were then, with their winter sport, already encroaching upon the short summers of our national game.

GRAFFHAM

The Leveret game may well have remained a one-off, had not over the following winter, a business associate, Alan Russell-Smith, introduced me to his father. He was President of a village cricket club at **Graffham** in Sussex. I was duly invited to bring a side down to the village that summer. Thus Jack Frost XI had a second fixture, all be it in season. I set about bringing together some of the original side, plus of course, Roger Hunt and a few more characters, including Bertie Bright who was for a while to become our regular wicket-keeper. It was an all day game on a Sunday, which was punctuated by the local vicar letting the Graffham batting side out of the church, overlooking the ground, in reverse order. This gave us a false sense of our own strength. Smith, very much the local squire, had laid on a grand spread for lunch, served by village maidens, in the Graffham Village Hall. Unfortunately the printed menus showed us visitors to be **Esher Cricket Club**, which led to much consternation from Esher cricketing star T.O.M.Simpson. After the speeches we returned to the game. Once again we came second.

The evening was perfect with a magnificent reception laid on at Mr. Smith's grand home. Tables were laden with home made country pates and pies, beer, wine and

I - FOUNDATION AND EARLY YEARS

spirits. We were invited to return the following year. An invitation we readily accepted for the next twenty five.

FORMALITIES

Much to our delight Jack Frost XI were asked to continue the end of season fixture with the Leverets. Thus by the end of 1962 we had completed three fixtures, still without a win. Now was the time to become more formalized and I decided a tie would suit us nicely. My memory threw up a character in the Rupert strip cartoon named Jack Frost. Finding a copy of the annual I was able to design a tie with a plain green ground, for the green sward, and a silver figure, for the frost. The Jack Frost XI tie was manufactured. A single tie was despatched to the Lord's Museum, where it is still displayed in a showcase of club ties, and further ties given to those who had played all three games. On the original tie the Jack Frost image had two arms but it since appears to have lost a limb.

I wrote up a constitution which had as its aim 'to extend the cricket season at both ends'. Subject to committee approval, an invitation and the playing of three games would constitute membership. We applied and joined the Club Cricket Conference, 'Surrey - Wandering' Section. A committee was gathered together, made up of such persons as Kim Morell, Alan Miller; then my brother-in-law; and a good all round player, another schoolmaster, Richard Greenwood and others. Thus with the 1963 approaching we were much enjoying our cricket and the club was now on a roll. Over the next few years further fixtures were added to the list and more cricketers invited to play for the XI. We sought to find opponents where we guessed we would have a good time in the bar after the game. As most of the serious cricket was played on Saturdays, it was decided to play our matches on Sundays when we would not be poaching our players from their regular clubs. The extended season games made available a host of worthy persons keen to play more cricket and of our kind.

OCKHAM

Following our policy of extending the season at both ends, we next obtained a fixture in April with **Ockham** Cricket Club, in a tiny village located off the main road between Ripley and Guildford. Overlooking the ground was The Hautboy, a first class hostelry. The fixture came about due to my milkman, Frank Arksey being linked with the Ockham club. Their top player was local lad Johnny Byrne who, besides being a more than useful cricketer, also played soccer for West Ham and went on to wear the England Football shirt. The wicket, as we were to learn in later fixtures, was somewhat agricultural but in very early 1963 the mud took the sting out of it. This match brought Jack Frost XI it's first victory and thus must be celebrated in the Public

I - FOUNDATION AND EARLY YEARS

Bar of the Hautboy, when I first introduced the treble scotch man of the match award. I believe it went to a young houseman at St.Georges Hospital, by the name of Nick Newton, who had kept wicket and scored a few runs.

We still play Ockham, which makes this match our longest running continuous fixture, and is still our first match of the season. The wicket has much improved over the past nearly forty years. Somewhat later the Hautboy was taken over and turned into a first-class restaurant by Jack Froster, Michael Watson-Smythe. Of him more later. Over the years, many fun evenings were had in the newly built Ockham Pavilion, where Frost played the inaugural opening game. One year the wife of their chairman did, without much persuasion, treat all to a streak around the ground. In the 1970's, Jack Frost XI did play a special match at Ockham to raise funds for one of their young players who lost his legs when he was crushed on his motorcycle by a a very drunken famous band leader. When Brad Bradley became Chairman of the XI, he chose the first game of the season, to hold his Chairman's Party. Much grub and booze for all.

During the 1980's, Canadian, Ron Tyrell was appointed Flag Master and set about raising the Frost flag on the newly provided mast alongside the refurbished pavilion. Unfortunately Ron had no naval or military experience in hoisting flags and did not understand ropes. He set about unbolting the flagpole from its setting, with the result that the brand new and previously unused mast tipped and fell to the ground smashing, not only into a million chips but, also demolishing a long line of, fortunately unoccupied, deck chairs. The later fracas Ron had with a dobermann pinscher did no harm to the dog, when Ron said to the owner, "I won't harm the little doggy" and got the reply "It's not the dog I am worried about". On one occasion in the 1970's Ockham kindly lent us their ground so we may play another friendly wandering club. **The Merton Alcoholics** had been founded by famed Old Rutlishian, David Willis then a Liberal Councillor for the Borough of Merton and formerly my brother in arms at Aldershot, Army Catering Corps Cook-Sargeant Willis.

This match was marked by the arrival of two of our players in evening dress, David Dandridge and Michael Welch. They had come straight from the celebration of the Centenary of Hockey, held by the games founders, Teddington Hockey Club. H.M.Queen Elizabeth II had provided swan and venison for the dinner at the Cafe Royal, but later sent in an invoice for several swans and a deer or two. By the time we played this match Jack Frost XI membership had expanded greatly with some seventy or so active qualified members. There was much competition for invitations to play. We already had a club flag and Sydney Smith designed a deerstalker cap, complete with a tank for beer and a tube to the mouth. After little deliberation Laurence Dillamore said he would get a proper cap, resulting in the Australian style floppy cap we now wear. By this time their was the odd person we wished to get rid of. It was at

I – FOUNDATION AND EARLY YEARS

this point that we introduced the no expulsion rule. We just lost their address.

Included amongst our regulars was a particular first class cricketer, one Saeed Hattea (Syd The Flying Wog). Syd was born in Bombay and educated at City of London School thus was introduced by Kim Morell. At this time he was then on the staff of **Gloucestershire C.C.C.** In 1970 he had in one day's post received two invitations to play. He did tell me that the invitation to play Frost cricket was the greater honour. I am not sure that I believed him as the other was to play for the Rest of The World against England at the Scarborough Festival. There, in his very fast opening spell, he dismissed three of the first four England batsmen, John Edrich, Peter Parfitt, Eric Russell and Brian Luckhurst. Earlier Syd had achieved notoriety by appearing at Lord's, representing the Public Schools against the School Masters, going out to bat with a cricket bat painted in bright phycodellic images. That was before he bowled the masters out, David C. Belchamber commenting that he was the fastest schoolboy he had ever faced.

Willis had produced a useful side including John Scott who was opening the bowling for leading Western League club, **Weston-super-Mare**, as well as turning out for Somerset II's. Jack Frost XI batted first on a very indifferent Ockham track and stood up well to Scott's pace attack even when he threw in more than a fair share of bouncers, particularly at our tail enders. When it was the turn for John Scott to face the bowling, it was the signal for the Flying Wog to mark out his run up to the sight screen. Body-line must be on the menu and a close field was set. Scott stood erect to face the demon. Syd ran in at frightening speed. A swift yorker demolished the stumps with Syd following through his run-up to put his face in front of the batsman, wagging his finger with the words, "You naughty boy". Honours were even. So it came about that I captained the Jack Frost XI through it's early years and saw it grow into a properly constituted and successful wandering cricket club.

Where it all Started
Hare Lane Green, Claygate, Surrey where the first Jack Frost XI cricket match was played against the Leveret Cricket Club on 8th October, 1961

The Swan Tavern, Claygate
Frosters and Leverets gather for libations outside the pub on Hare Lane Green. The last of thirty games between the two clubs was held in October 1990 after which the Leveret Cricket Club folded.

Chapter II – THE FIRST TOUR AND ONWARD

Due to the growing numbers of cricketers wishing to play the social cricket we offered, a number of new fixtures were added to the Jack Frost XI list, over the nest few seasons. As a wandering side, without ground upkeep, it was incumbent that we socialised with the opposition so as to help their bar turnover. We were beginning to gain quite a reputation as a club who played good social cricket and had a fearsome bar reputation. We were readily entertained by such clubs as the **Artisans** in Surbiton, **Old Citizens, Avorians, Norwood, The Crickets** and other assorted outfits who were introduced to us.

NEW FOREST TOURS

An important feature of the club's development came about when regular player Alan Miller moved to take up residence at Netherbrook House in Ringwood, Hampshire there to conduct his antiques business. Alan started to play cricket for the local **Ringwood Cricket Club** on the Carvers Cricket Ground, in the centre of the town.

Soon he suggested that we bring down a Jack Frost XI for an extended weekend tour, with fixtures against Ringwood plus Burley up in the Forest. Other matches were added including **New Milton**, who through Peter Cooper had strong ties to the **Hampshire County Cricket Club** and they often turned out county players such as 'Butch' White. The most memorable incident at New Milton came about when we had accumulated a decent score and our bowlers had them on the rack. I decided to introduce leg-spin in the large shape of Jimmy O'Connor. We did not take another wicket as Jimmy was thrashed around the large ground. It was on this occasion that H.Sydney Smith made his memorable comment about my "having snatched defeat from the jaws of victory". The New Milton captain, Peter Cooper was also a much respected Motor- Rally Steward for the R.A.C. Soon Chris Horner was espousing his rally experience and spoke so forcefully that Peter appointed him as his navigator, for the Eire Rally. Unfortunately Peter, who had previously never failed to appear in the first three, was penalised a thousand points for entering the wrong country, when Chris inadvertently led him across the border into Ulster.

Later the other Ringwood club, **Picket Post** was added to the list with one famous game against a little club, **Downton** on the road to Stockbridge. A memory of the Downton game was the picture of Tony Denning strolling, alongside the sunlit River Avon, hand in hand with a beautiful blonde maiden, who had come down with another Frost member. It was here that when their dishevelled, hick, teenage opening bowler castled Kim Morell, first ball of the match. Kim marched up to the kid and asked for his name as he needed to pass it onto Lord's, as "You should be playing cricket for England". The evening of this match was enlivened by the presence in our side of a Jamaican, Johnny Millington, who was Alan Miller's chauffeur. As Downton

II - THE FIRST TOUR AND ONWARD

lies alongside the Hampshire Avon their is a famous anglers public house known for its fresh water fish where we arranged dinner. Adorned in a polished Life Guard helmet complete with horsehair tassels, Johnny entertained us with impromptu Caribbean piano and songs. Unfortunately the landlord transpired to be a retired Guards Colonel who did not take kindly to Johnny limbo dancing in his regimental head-gear and we were required to leave.

WIMBORNE

The cricket club at **Wimborne Minster** is in the centre of the Dorset town, but a short drive from our Ringwood Tour headquarters. The ground is used for Minor County matches with a good wicket and very fast outfield. After the New Forest tour had come to an end we, for a number of years, retained this prime fixture. A memorable incident at Wimborne occurred when Brian Rhodes bowled a medium pace long hop at their leading batsman. He hit the ball a mighty blow straight onto the head of Tony Clarke, who had moved in close. He's mad you know, and already had a metal plate in his head from a rugby injury. Babs was poleaxed and taken by ambulance unconsciously to hospital. However, with great presence of mind, Brian Rhodes continued his run and caught the ball off Clarke's head. The poor batsman concerned about the life of the man he had struck was nonplussed when declared out, caught and bowled. At close of play all awaited news from the hospital when Clarke, having discharged himself, strolled across the ground, entered the pavilion and immediately downed a pint of bitter.

Our drinking headquarters in Ringwood was a back alley pub, the Smiths Arms. It was very tiny and did not have any customers. As we put large quantities of cash into their till the landlord, and his good wife Bonny, were only too pleased to allow the Frosters carte blanche. It was here that we learnt about 'Earthquakes'. A rare pub customer was a 'Scouser' who had spent time as a Steward on the cruise liners between Liverpool and New York. He gave us the recipe for jugs made up of one bottle of gin, one of brandy topped up with bitter lemon and lemonade, which were poured into sugar-coated champagne glasses. A suitable sauce which we adopted as the club drink and for many a year served this potent mix to both our opponents and ourselves. On tour we always drank a jug, or two, of Earthquakes before every game. The other pub customer was the licence's nephew, a gregarious young man under the name of Joe Geary, who claimed to know everyone in the town. He explained he had a top job with the gas board and was thus able to spend a lot of his time in pubs. This myth was burst when we later saw him operating a red "Stop" and green "Go" sign to direct road traffic around the gas pipe laying.

When the tour had extended to five or six games we decided to allow wives,

II - THE FIRST TOUR AND ONWARD

girlfriends and mistresses to join us from the Friday evening onward. We stayed in a series of different hotels in the area, none for too long. It was at the "Crown Hotel" in Ringwood that, after his third year on tour, Alan Hawtin signed in with his "wife", the receptionist remarking, 'Ah, the third Mrs. Hawtin. I believe'. The pub where we eventually settled was "The Star" in the market place in Ringwood. The landlord was a delightful local character, Cyril Browning. He did a bit of local broadcasting, with a soft Hampshire burr not unlike John Arlott, and played a lot of golf, where he found no shortage of Frost partners. His bar attraction with a vast quantity and variety of malt and grain whiskeys. On at least one tour Kim Morell won Cyril's bet that he could not go through the card of different brands. At an hotel in Burley, after a late night walk in the adjoining woods, Valerie Martin rushed white faced into the bar claiming to have seen a ghost. Brian bravely went out to lay the apparition only to find that a pile of horse droppings were evaporating gasses which in the freezing atmosphere materialized as a ghostly figure.

At the "Everglades Hotel" in Lyndhurst, the owner explained to Chris Horner that he was an international bowler. After many hours searching through 'Wisden', Horner challenged the publican who explained he was a ten-pin bowler. At Ringwood's "Avon Hotel", "My Name is Jack" proved to be the tour song, but Pammy the manageress, who knew the beat, provided most of the entertainment. Another fabled character at **Ringwood Cricket Club** was Nobby Clarke. He introduced himself as an antique dealer but in reality dipped pine furniture into acid baths to sell to vulnerable young married couples. Nobby was captain of Ringwood II's and in the early days ran the mid-week side against us. His most memorable match was when he took his side onto the field with three padded up wicket keepers, including himself, and no match ball. Soon Paul Ravera, the Ringwood 1st XI Captain took charge of the games against Frost. We used to beat Ringwood until they introduce Fazal Mahmood into their side. He was initially unrecognised, until the eagle eyed Chris Horner revealed their secret weapon to be the former Pakistani Test Cricketer.

Later Ringwood introduced the famed David "Pongo" Percy, who was a real executive of the Gas Board and skiperd Hampshire IInd XI. Pongo was also a genuine fast bowler so we soon found a place for him in Jack Frost XI. Unfortunately he soon resigned after Michael Copleston suggested that he was a faster and better bowler than Pongo. This was on the occasion we introduced true democracy into team selection by means of the single transferable vote.

JOHN EDRICH'S BENEFIT MATCH

During the year of John Edrich's benefit, Ringwood allowed us the use of the Carvers to hold a match in aid of the Edrich Benefit Fund. Lionel and Michael Citroen brought

II – THE FIRST TOUR AND ONWARD

down a side which included Peter May and the Bedser twins. Frost recruited John Edrich, Bill Smith and Roger Harmer all in the current Surrey County side. In the dressing room it was somewhat disconcerting to see the Bedser twins dressing from the same cricket bag, all their clobber being interchangeable.

Frost made a reasonable score, although John Edrich totalled only seven runs, which proved to be one more than the six he scored against New Zealand in the Test Match the following day. Batting at my usual number eleven, I managed to frustrate the opposition by, on the first ball, leg glancing Alec Bedser to the boundary. May and the Bedsers went into a huddle to work out how to dismiss me. They must never had considered bowling me a straight one. However the end came when the unfortunate Mr. Horner, at the other end, was bowled soon after. When Mr. Peter May batted, I without any difficulty managed to drop him. Mr. P.B.H.May went on to make a lot of runs and The Citroen's won the game before generously hosting a most excellent dinner at the Ferndown Hotel. The small village of **Burley**, who played on a small square cut out of forest heathland, was one of our earliest fixtures and the firmest of friends. Many of our favourite games were played against that village. Simon Rowley, then a young free lance press photographer, became our leading contact and was soon recruited into Frost. As a tearaway fast bowler he sprayed the ball around and when batting could score a lightning fifty.

Following one of the later tours we left Ringwood, early on a Saturday morning and headed to Kennington Oval. We had there a fixture with **Cricket Club of Geneva**, to be played under first-class rules. It was quite exciting for Jack Frost XI to walk through the pavilion and occupy the home dressing room. We had selected, from the whole club, the best side we could put on the field. Some of the players had been on the tour, others came directly from their homes. Club Captain, Tony Gill was not pleased when having lost the toss he at 11o'clock took the side onto the field two men short. Mike Ruffle was deputised to keep wicket as the chosen keeper David Cullen together with opening bowler Michael Copleston, turned up late. Not a good start. The weather was boiling hot and on the large field at the Oval our side were soon beginning to wilt. After an hour Mr.Gill signalled to the dressing room balcony for drinks to be brought out. This appeal received a shaking of the head from Frost 12th Man, Chris Horner.

Furious the captain ran to the boundary and ordered Horner to get the drinks out. Horner replied that he was no longer Frost 12th Man and Geneva were one short. Claiming to qualify for Geneva, he probably owned the bank, he was thus playing against Frost. Only the diplomacy of Roger Hunt prevented Gill from killing him there and then. The opposition, who seemed to be anything but Swiss, mostly English, Australians, South Africans to a man kept Frost running around the vast playing area

II – THE FIRST TOUR AND ONWARD

as they piled on runs. Mr.Gill foolishly put himself on to bowl, on a wicket that failed to help turn the ball an inch, found Jimmy Cook on strike. He has no memory of the rest of the spell, after the first ball was struck over the boundary, the perimeter wall, the road, a double decker bus and landed in the playground of the Archbishop Tennyson School. The caretaker had to be summoned to retrieve the ball. After Bob Hurst had in great heat, bowled a marathon spell to keep them quite, he remarked that was why he gave up first-class cricket, with Middlesex. Geneva scored a lot of runs and Jack Frost XI did not get enough.

The only joy came when the Frost dressing room balcony became crowded to enjoy watching Chris Horner sweat it out chasing the ball around the Oval cover boundary. Some lady supporters, Jill Copleston and others, were true to form when they went to Lord's to watch the match. They were surprised by the number of spectators on the ground where England were playing a Test Match. Tony Gill laid on a barbecue for the teams at his Esher home but none of the opposition, except Horner, turned up thus leaving more for Frost to enjoy. When the match was reported in The Daily Telegraph the Cricket Club of Geneva denied all knowledge of the game. The Oval match was a great experience for Jack Frost XI and would only be topped if we were to get a game at Lord's.

NEW YEAR MATCHES

For many years after the full New Forest tours finished we still kept our association with **Burley** through our New Year's Day games. We started these events by taking a party of Frosters, wives, girlfriends, mistresses and friends to stay the long New Year holidays in a local hotel. Always a good dinner was held on the eve of New Year followed by a match against Burley, on matting the following day. Peter Probyn (P.J.), David Dandridge, Michael Welch and umpire Chris Clayton were regulars for New Year. At first we stayed at the White Buck Country Hotel near the ground, which was managed by Jack Frost member, Steve Bowyer. Unfortunately, one year Steve was sacked at midnight on New Years eve. That year we not only provided the cabaret but also reduced the bar stock to nil. We did cook the other guest breakfast. This was followed by the smart Stag Hotel in Lymington where the wife of a doctor member did a most erotic striptease in the bar at midnight. Then an even smarter Country House Hotel, again in Burley.

The most famous New Year's match was played in a year when it snowed heavily over the holiday. The B.B.C sports unit faced cancelled racing and soccer and took the opportunity to film our match to lead their New Year's Day "Sports Grandstand". Photographs of the game appeared on the front page of the "Daily Telegraph" and in newspapers in South Africa, Israel and elsewhere.

II – THE FIRST TOUR AND ONWARD

A unique aspect of the early New Forest tours was the generous parties we were able to throw for ourselves, our opponents and friends. Alan Miller having a large Queen Anne house, a tithe barn and appropriate grounds we were able, through his kindness, to host grand parties. The film "Tom Jones" was popular at the time of our first tour. It was decided to hold a fancy dress do in the mode of Henry Fielding's romp. Gentlemen dressed in swashbuckling XVIIIth Century costume mingled on the lawn with Ladies in revealing low cut gowns. A period stagecoach served as the bar, staffed by the most attractive French wife of one of our members. Large quantities of beer were consumed as it was necessary for the amply chested young lady to bend very low to serve, from barrels of beer, through the window. In the barn a whole lamb was roasted over a spit. At midnight, as the doves were released from the dovecote, the grounds were thrown into floodlight, revealing a guest urinating against an ancient statue of Pan.

The following morning a horse race was run on a training ground in the forest, with a golden guinea as a prize. I managed to beat former 10th Hussar Alan Russell-Smith, over a measured mile, and claim the prize. Due mainly to a number of falls, although the race was on the flat, other Frosters did not enter the frame. Earlier on the tour, a morning Frost Golf Tournament had taken place at the nine hole Burley Golf Club. In later years similar tournaments were held at Brockenhurst Golf Club. The following year the party theme was "Dick Turpin" held in similar vein to the original event. Many more members came for the night to Ringwood to swell the guest list. Another memorable moment in Ringwood came when that magnificent man Robin Needham, doyen of **Old Emmanuel**, fell in love with a barmaid. We arranged a press conference on the lawn at Netherbrook House, where Robin, forgetting both her indoors and his young son Patrick nestling at his home in Surrey, announced his engagement to his new love. The local papers made great play on the famous cricketer from London who came to Ringwood and became engaged to a local girl.

It took a lot of diplomacy, on the part of Alan Hawtin, to put matters to rights. The New Forest tours went a long way in developing the spirit of Frost cricket during the season and proved popular for a decade.

MIDLANDS TOURS

Due to the popularity of the New Forest Tours, which were held in June, it was decided, so as to accommodate the schoolmaster and student membership, to add an August tour to the list. Roger Hunt, who then taught at Milbourne Lodge Preparatory School, hailed from Redditch in Worcestershire. Roger volunteered to put together a tour in and around Worcestershire and Warwickshire. Thus in the late sixties we set off to lodge at the private hotel run by Ms. Margaret Jones, according to the local

II - THE FIRST TOUR AND ONWARD

paper; aged 26. She was over fifty if she was a day, but tried hard to dress and act 26. The fact that, as far as I know, not one of the tourists fancied her is to say enough.

An unusual aspect of her bar was that as we finished a bottle of spirits, Ms. Jones had to nip out to the off-licence to replenish with the cash sales to date. She made many such trips during our stay at her hotel. The social highlight, of the first tour, was the trial of Billy Reynolds. It was decided to trump up some charge against popular tourist and swing bowler Billy Reynolds. A court was set up in the bar of the hotel, with Arthur Hammond appointed as Judge and Tony (Babs) Clarke as Clerk of the Court. Various other tourists were appointed as Prosecution and Defence lawyers, etc, with the members of **Redditch Cricket Club** as the Jury. Great amusement was generated as the kangaroo court proceeded. There was never a verdict as the Jury were locked in a bedroom to consider their verdict and the key went missing, (What did you do with it Copleston?) leaving the jury to spend the night in the room.

The Midlands Tours soon became a breeding ground for young Jack Frost XI talent.

A number of sons, brothers and friends of Frosters at university and the like had the time in August to play mid-week cricket. Furthermore our schoolmaster members introduced boys making the transition between school and club cricket. A number of youngsters from **Epsom College, Reeds School** and other schools were introduced to Frost on this tour, with some going on to be long term members. Generally speaking the standard of cricket was markedly higher than that in the New Forest. Established clubs as **Redditch**, **Kingsheath** (Birmingham League), and **Studley** formed the core of the fixtures with from time to time various others added. Norman Grey, Gerry Wilkinson and others from **Pearl Assurance** toured regularly in the Midlands. We were treated to great hospitality wherever we went in the Midlands. One of the most picturesque grounds was that at Ragley Hall, home of Viscount Newport. The playing area overlooked by the grand manor house and the grounds populated by sheep.

Redditch Cricket Club were our main hosts, and besides good games of cricket to a reasonably fair standard, they looked after us well in the bar. We always won the boat race, especially when Robin Crawford ate his glass . On the early tours Studley was a regular fixture with the evenings enlivened by great plates of local dish faggots and mushy peas. The downside of this fixture was the presence in the opposition of Brian Buffrey. He was a West Midlands policeman with a most aggressive personality both on and off the field. After about three years we decided we could no longer put up with Buffrey and duly obtained a fixture with a strong village side **Astwood Bank**. They had just reached the final of the Village Knock-Out and had composed a song for their visit to Lord's. "Astwood Bank, Astwood Bank only came here for a wank", which one wonders how this ditty went down in the Long Room. Upon arriving at the Astwood Bank ground I knocked on the home side dressing room door to find their

II – THE FIRST TOUR AND ONWARD

captain for the toss. A voice rang out, 'Hullo Tony'. It was indeed the dreaded Buffrey who had changed clubs, in his words so that he could play against Jack Frost.

The games against **Kingsheath** were excellent. This Birmingham League side played on a charming ground surrounded by the well kept gardens of the adjacent houses, all of which was an oasis of luxury set in the middle of a very depressed area of Birmingham. At Kingsheath we faced many top quality club cricketers who generally proved too strong for Frost. The most memorable incident at Kingsheath was the parallel running between the wickets of Hiam and Simon Martineau. Things were drawing to an end for the Midlands Tour when we had to move our base to the Cherry Trees Motel. Unfortunately they did not understand cricket tourists and were most upset when Robin Crawford, whilst dragging a bed across the roof, put his foot through the ceiling of a chalet occupied by a honeymoon couple. A near riot followed and we were ejected for the offence of throwing a Gideon Bible out of the window. Roger Hunt, who did so much to make our visits to the Midlands so enjoyable, soothed matters over with the management. By then that tour had come to a natural end, somewhere in the early 1970's.

OVER THE SEA TO IRELAND

As an American astronaut by the name of Neil Armstrong took a great step for man, Jack Frost XI were taking a great step into Irish cricket by arriving at Belfast Airport, moon-dancing off the flight. The Ulster Tour was the brainchild of the Citroen Brothers, Lionel and Michael. Through the good auspices of Belfast banker, Brian White, they had set up a series of fixtures in the Provence. What we had not realised was that the internal political timing, July 1969, was not good. The first murmurs of the more recent troubles were beginning to rise to the surface, which with hindsight we know to have been so distressing. We were accommodated at the "Wellington Hotel", which was later to be bombed on any number of occasions. At that time the hotel was of a good standard and a most comfortable billet for the tour party of some eighteen or more. As tour captain, I was allocated the room occupied by Garfield Sobers, during the famous West Indies visit to Sion Mills. After visiting the Guinness Brewery and Bushmills Distillery, the Windies suffered the only defeat of their tour.

I was assured they had changed the sheets. A taste of what was to come came when Kim ordering a sandwich enquired if the beef was rare? The waiter, looking scathingly at Kim, replied "It depends how long you cook it". The Citroens were, besides being Jack Frost XI members, also associated with **The Park Cricket Club** which was centred in and around Ealing. For this tour, the brothers introduced a number of Park members to Frost. Roy Furness, David Lidgate, Erskine Holder, Lyn Myers, Mike Turner, Mike Ruffle, Eric Wilson and others joined us for the trip. The first fixture was

II – THE FIRST TOUR AND ONWARD

against the famous Old Boys, the **Instonians**. The game ended in a draw. Next day took us to **Woodvale**, a club deeply entrenched in the heart of Protestant Belfast. After a very hard game, Frost came out winners. The following day we made a trip down to the Mountains of Mourne, with a view to playing golf at the Royal Belfast Golf Club at Newcastle, County Down. After a very expensive sandwich lunch at the famous Slieve Donan Hotel, most of the party went onto the course.

Deciding not to move from the comfortable hotel lounge bar, Alan Hawtin, Lyn Myers, Mike Turner and myself decided to refresh ourselves. The order was the same every time, each of us taking it in turn to request a bottle of Verve Clequot, four pints of Guinness and four large Bushmill Whiskey's. After a round each, there entered the bar a familiar face needing refreshing after his eighteen holes. Noting our foursome, by now in very good form, Sean Connery entered the spirit of the afternoon by ordering the same round and joining our party. That evening Jack Frost XI were to be entertained to dinner by the Ulster Cricket Union at the Hollywood Hotel. It took some two hours in a hot bath before Mr. Gill was able to respond to the toast. The following day was the prime fixture when we were to meet **North of Ireland** on their ground, a miniature version of Lord's, in the centre of Belfast.

I was awoken by the hotel staff informing me that a Doctor Sonny Hole was awaiting me for breakfast. I duly went down to meet one of the most delightful persons I have ever met on a cricket tour. Sonny was a most respected man in sporting and medical circles. Besides being educated at Trinity, Dublin he had captained both Ireland and Israel at cricket and was my opposite number for the forthcoming match commencing at 11am. Awaiting me on the breakfast table were jugs of Guinness and Irish Whisky which he and I willingly consumed. At nine thirty Dr. Hole made his departure, excusing himself as he had to visit a few patients before the game. Unfortunately the game suffered from early curtailment due to a massive rain storm which flooded the ground. However, the North had in the evening organised a Grande Hooley. In our innocence, we did put up our foot in it by inviting, what proved to be a Republican, folk band to entertain. Songs of "Rifles Clashing" did not go down well in the strictly Protestant clubhouse. The last game saw us at the ground of **Queens University**, Belfast. John Isaacs had produced an experimental cricket ball, orange in colour.

The University kindly agreed to our playing with this unusual ball. Only when opening swing bowler, Mike Turner, complained that he could not bowl a banana with an orange did we revert to the usual plumb coloured sphere. We did win that game. It was at the end of this game that we telephoned **Normandy** in Surrey and the Midlands to ascertain how the other two Jack Frost XI sides had fared that day. It was around the late sixties and early seventies that the XI was probably at its strongest playing

II - THE FIRST TOUR AND ONWARD

most Sundays, many mid-week games and undertaking three tours per season. Such was the friendship we made in and around Belfast that the Ulstermen asked Jack Frost XI to organise their future tours of England. A couple of years later we arranged fixtures for them in and around Surrey besides playing them ourselves at Esher Cricket Club. Unfortunately, despite much negotiation, they were unable to host us and were themselves unable to undertake another tour to the mainland due their players being unwilling to leave their wives and families alone in the then strife torn province.

THE EMERALD ISLE - ONCE MORE

Politically our next excursion across the Irish Sea was in 1970. We pragmatically chose County Cork in the Republic of Ireland for our invasion. Our welcome was assured when having landed at Cork Airport, the most fog shrouded part of the Irish coast, we were met by Danny our coach driver for the tour. Danny instructed us to put our "cricket sticks in the baggage hold" before he took us on a sight-seeing tour of the city. The driver took us the best part of one hundred yards out of the airport before swerving across a dual carriageway and coming to halt outside a pub. "The first thing you must learn is the Guinness", Danny thereupon ordered twenty seven pints, for a party of 25 and downed the first and the last to be poured.

Next we visited Cork Industrial Estate where Danny showed us the Ford factory, explaining that it was the "Biggest in the World". Sitting behind the driver, Lionel Citroen enquired what they made? "Henry Ford and Son. They make motor cars." came the reply, "You see a lot of them around Ireland, they have their name Ford on the back. Henry runs the factory in America and his son the one here in Cork." Our next visit was to Blarney Castle where Robin Crawford was the first to bend backwards over the huge open drop to kiss the Blarney Stone. A few Frosters followed his example, but not the captain. The following day saw our fixture against **Cork County Cricket Club** on the famous Mardyke. The intense pace of Duncan 'Mickey' Carmichael decimated the Irish and resulted in a swift Jack Frost XI victory. The awards ceremony had a very Irish flavour. The Cork captain, Pat Duneen, congratulated Jack Frost XI on their victory over Cork County 2nd XI. On enquiring where the 1st XI were, he replied that we had in fact played their first eleven but they had called themselves the 2nd XI just in case we won. Which just goes to show you can't beat the Irish on their home ground.

A coach journey with the leprechaun, Danny, headed us towards Waterford. A one pound sweep amongst Frosters revealed twenty three examples of "The Biggest in the World" from our unaware driver. Our instruction was to meet in the main Waterford Hotel, in the high street. Upon our arrival we were told by the management that we

II - THE FIRST TOUR AND ONWARD

could not come in as the whole hotel was booked for a big reception. After lunching in a local pub we found the ground, at a local school. Awaiting us was an angry local magistrate who introduced himself as Chairman of **Waterford Cricket Club**. He was not pleased at our not turning up for the reception he had organised, at the hotel we had been refused entry. The big reception, to which the management had referred, had been for us. Frost having arrived on time for a two o'clock start were then made to wait some two hours for the arrival of the opposition. Eventually a figure approached waving his arms and reciting loudly the work of William Butler Yates. The Chairman introduced this person as both their local poet and Captain of Waterford C.C.

I expressed my disappointment at having a late start. His reply was devastatingly Irish. "Isn't better that we start at four o'clock with the sun shining than at two o'clock with the rain pouring down". As it was a beautiful day with no sign of rain, I pointed out that it had not rained at 2 o'clock. "Never mind that. It might have been raining. We can start soon, anyway", came the devastating reply. We managed to win the match with ease, not having the need to call upon the bowling of Mickey Carmichael. We repaired to the Waterford Hotel, a grand establishment on the waterfront, where our opponents had not only laid on a splendid dinner but also laid on a dance band. Our host, their President, was an ancient, certainly in his eighties, if not a decade older, who instructed the waiter to keep on serving whisky to himself and myself whenever our glass was empty. Our glasses were often empty.

Our final match of the tour was against a combined **South of Ireland** team, at a venue miles from anywhere. This match was memorable for the fact they wished us to make it a timeless two innings match. As they were again exceedingly late in arriving we were anxious to get on with the game. "Don't worry about time. If it gets dark we can continue tomorrow", they extolled. I explained we were flying home the next day. "Don't worry about that as the airport will be fogged up tomorrow." In the event Carmichael did the business, poleaxed their leading bat, an International Irish cricketer and bowled out the South of Ireland with little difficulty in very few overs. The following day, we arrived at a fog bound Cork Airport, after Danny had stopped, several times on route to order twenty seven pints of Guinness and explaining the, "airaplane would not be there because of the Irish mist". At least the Irish were right about the weather. We had enjoyed a most successful tour to the Republic and come out with three out of three victories.

Opening Pair
Jack Frost XI opening batsmen, M.V.G.Copleston and W.A.Smith, walk out to bat on the Carvers in the 1968 game against the Citroen XI, in aid of the John Edrich Benefit Fund.
John Edrich, through his binoculars watching Mike Copleston bat, later asked "Why is that chap not playing County Cricket?".

Jack Frost XI v The Citroen XI Ringwood 1968
Back row Jack Frost XI, from left: Keith Ives, Roger Macness, Chris Horner, Michael Copleston, Geoff Chichester (Wk), Bill Reynolds, Tony Gill (Capt) Alan Hawtin, Roger Harman, John Edrich, Bill Smith.
Front row Citroen XI from centre left: Lionel and Michael Citroen, Alec Bedser, Peter May and Eric Bedser.

Chapter III – MID-WEEK FROSTING

By the early seventies Jack Frost XI were prepared to take on a number of stronger clubs, playing these clubs mainly in their cricket weeks. We by this time had a membership in the region of one hundred, many of them good club cricketers who were available to play mid-week.

We had also introduced the Match Manager system for getting the sides out, with the manager usually skippering the XI. The rule had been introduced that sides should include at least eight members with up to three places available for those under qualification. If a fellow was found to be acceptable on social grounds he was usually invited to play in a third qualifying game, after which he was to down a treble scotch and was allowed to wear the club regalia, cap on the field and tie in civies. As well as paying a subscription. Qualification depended on the probationer being a good guy and as many cricket duffers were accepted as stars were rejected.

ESHER CRICKET CLUB

As a number of our members were **Esher C.C.** players we were, by the late sixties fortunate, to obtain a fixture, in their prestigious Cricket Week. The wicket and outfield at Esher are first-class with excellent pavilion, changing facilities and bar. The groundsman was a young Christopher Woods who is now the English and Welsh Cricket Board wicket inspector. Initially James Parker captained Esher against Frost and the opposition usually contained such regulars as Jamie Allen-Smith and the young Bobby Lowe, an all-rounder who regularly played Surrey Two cricket. Their President was the great Peter Wreford who was generous in providing decanters of port after lunch. Jack Frost added a new dimension by providing chilled white port before the games. The Esher sides were initially much stronger than Frost, which changed by the time we had Peter Murray and later Lance Keen managing our side. Lance, in particular, usually made a point of making a big score against Esher. A long boozy session was always certain after the Esher games, with many jugs of gin and tonic making the rounds.

So as to provide extended evening entertainment for the many members who came to watch the cricket in the evenings during Cricket Week, they at one time organised a six-a-side knock-out competition with teams from local clubs, such as **Claygate**, **Thames Ditton** and elsewhere. One year Frost were fortunate to reach the final, which we lost to an Esher side. This was partly due to the fact that on the Friday Final we turned out a full eleven against **Turnham Green** that day and not expecting to make such progress we had to turn out a rather scratch six for the final.

III – MID-WEEK FROSTING

TEDDINGTON

Michael Peter Redmayne Welsh, who has now been the führer of **Teddington Cricket Club** for some years and David Dandridge amongst others were involved regularly with Jack Frost cricket. It was therefore natural that we should meet Teddington in their week. Teddington generally turned out what was basically their Second Eleven strengthened by a few first team players including the likes of Ted Clarke and Bob Hurst, both formerly of Middlesex. Bob went onto become a Frost member with his left armers often proved invaluable for the XI.

The Teddington ground, the most prestigious of the five clubs playing within Bushy Park; the others being **Teddington Town, Hampton, Hampton Wick Royal**, also at that time a Frost fixture in their week, and **National Physical Laboratory** a recent Frost fixture. A then new pavilion sits neatly overlooking a large playing area with the grand vista of the Royal Park, complete with deer, an idyllic back-drop. Many hard fought games were played during our Teddington week games and many Teddington players over the years came to play Frost cricket. These included Chris Wilson who has for some years now managed the Frost match against Tilford. For any number of years we were fed by Welch's mother, Mona, who home cooked most excellent curries. Mad antics took place in the pavilion with our very strong boat-race team, more often than not, winning the evening games. When Jack Frost XI played, M.P.R.Welch usually took the precaution of fixing the park gate-keepers so as to ensure that the players were not locked in at sundown.

OXSHOTT

Oxshott Village Cricket Club was one of our first Cricket Week fixtures, where we made many friends. Some thirty years later, we still play this most sociable club and much enjoy their hospitality Their ground is spacious and includes a Squash Court in the well equipped pavilion with adjacent tennis courts and room for such sports as archery. Some of their members became Jack Frosters including the very valuable left-arm medium pace bowler, Chis Crowhurst. His son Alistair a good all-rounder is now a leading member of Frost, as well as currently being Frost's Honorary Club Secretary. The most valued acquisition from Oxshott must be the present Jack Frost XI Chairman, David Lipop who, besides playing regularly, is a most hard working administrator and fixture secretary. A particular aspect of the Oxshott games is that, the sides usually being well matched, they are inducive to good cricket resulting in often tight finishes. This is much due to the example set by the original match manager, Roger Hunt, who together with his family, lives in the village. The Oxshott club always lay on a good feast after the game thus encouraging a good sociable evening.

III – MID-WEEK FROSTING

HAMPTON WICK ROYAL
The friendly **Hampton Wick Royal Cricket Club**, situated at the Kingson-on-Thames end of Bushy Park, was a popular fixture. The only problem with their Cricket Week games was that they often overestimated our strength and thus were reluctant to declare. This may have been due to our occasionally including the odd Warwickshire County cricketer in our team, to say nothing of Bob Hurst, formerly of Middlesex C.C.C., who if he did not bowl sides out, could at least tie up one end with his left-arm bowling. It was not often we came near to beating Hampton Wick Royal. It was at this venue that Bob Beeney presented the club with a John Newbury bat covered in blue plastic. It had been used as a display prop in a fashion boutique, but was never the less a fine bat, much used by our batsmen. Whatever the result we always had a wild party, after the game, when they generally laid on a band and/or a barbecue.

TWICKENHAM
Always a friendly all day game on the Green at Twickenham was very much a Jack Frost XI favourite. The home side were a sociable lot and the cricket was of a reasonable standard with both sides usually of equal strength. The Banks family were always in evidence. Michael Welch usually managed to supply a good quantity of port which was much enjoyed after the splendid lunches **Twickenham C.C.** provided during their Cricket Week. On one classic occasion D.P.Dandridge captaining Frost put Mr. Gill onto bowl the last over before lunch. It was a hot day and the port flowed over lunch. So much so that Dorothy took a gentle after lunch nap in a deckchair outside the pavilion. The players went out, sans skipper, and Gill continued his bowling spell. When awakened from his slumbers some long time later, D.P.D. was horrified to find that a lot of runs had gone onto the board but no wickets had fallen. During the early seventies we also had a number of mid-week games with strong league sides playing social cricket.

BRONDESBURY
Brondesbury, a strong Middlesex League side, is set in the middle of darkest North London, with a large sports ground, very difficult to find. On one occasion I was fortunate to bowl one of their openers, when much to my chagrin they sent in a sixteen year-old lad. Feeling hurt about this insult, I determined to make the same delivery as the previous wicket taking ball. It did not have the same effect as the groundsman had to be summoned to unlock the nearby tennis court, to retrieve the match ball. It transpired the young upstart was one Mike Gatting, who went on to greater things. All was well in the evening when I helped him close up the clubhouse, his parents the club stewards having left earlier. Relationships with Brondesbury reached a low when

III – MID-WEEK FROSTING

for lunch they served very scraggy over cooked chicken. The club caterer did not share the joke when Michael Welch awarded him the Man of the Match Award. This was compounded when the following year, Michael arranged for Harrod's to deliver him a food hamper at lunch-time. However, he did offer the Brondesbury captain, Martin Edney, a quails egg.

OLD EPSOMIANS

We were included into the **Old Epsomians** Cricket Week by Froster Robin Crawford, both an old boy of Epsom College and the old boy's caterer during the week they took over the delightful school ground for their festival. This match proved to be most civilized with a proffered glass of port prior to the toss, a good standard of cricket, first class wine at lunch and a barbecue after the match. The Old Eposomians have a good cricket tradition and despite Babs Clarke bowling them out on the odd occasion and West Indian Test Cricketer and Jack Frost member Reg Scarlett scoring runs and taking wickets, we have had and still do have any number of close games. During the mid-seventies we were playing about thirty fixtures per season, mainly Sundays and mid-week. Our membership had risen to some one hundred and thirty members. Numbers of new fixtures had, due to Frost's popularity, been added to the list. Some of these matches proved to be one off.

Froster Dick Tindell introduced a fixture, with strong Surrey club, **East Molesey**, which proved to be a singular event. The Friday was over clouded and it did not take long for the rains to fall. Jack Frost were skippered by Roger Kingdon who's opposite number was John Bamber. When we dashed to the pavilion, in a downpour, we were impressed at the speed and efficiency of the ground staff in covering the wicket. When the rain ceased and the sun came out strongly we prepared to take our place in the field. However, the umpires declared the wicket unfit for play. The air turned blue when we discovered East Molesey had, in fact, covered the wicket next to the one we were currently using, as they wished to protect the wicket for the next day's league match. John Bamber refused our request for an apology at what we considered an insult and despite Dick Tindell's attempt at cooling things down, by buying drinks for all taking part in the game, we dropped that fixture. It may also have had something to do with one of their player's hairpiece becoming damaged and then removed during the three man lift.

Things did not go well from the start of our singular match with **Malden Wanderers**. They were at that time quite a force in Surrey cricket and included the South African Test player, Russell Endean. Malden rather looked down on Frost and even before the toss challenged the Grade 'A' ball we had provided. Their next request was for the game to finish early due to a World Cup Soccer match on television. This

III – MID-WEEK FROSTING

was naturally refused. In the event, Frost's first four batsmen, Roger Hunt, Martin Danford, Michael Copleston and one other, made individual scores of over fifty. Malden were not best pleased when Tony 'Babs' Clarke bowled them out. The atmosphere in the pavilion deteriorated from bad to impossible when Copleston literally pulled the plug from their television set when they tried to watch soccer. We dropped that fixture.

By this time we had, through the introduction of Robin Needham, a good number of Old Emmanuel C.C. members. These included Robin's talented son Patrick Needham, David Debidin and Peter Sawyer, who had toured with Frost in the New Forest. Peter celebrated his Twenty-First Birthday, on tour by chuntering into Copleston's cricket bag. It was therefore natural that we should play mid-week matches at Blagdons against **Old Emmanuel**.

One of the first Surrey Hills mid-week fixtures was in the cricket week of **Blackheath C.C.**, a tiny little village with a naturally beautiful ground cut out of the woodland. Many good games were and still are played here. Much later, 1975, we introduced the great hitter, Don Weeks to Frost for this game. John, the Blackheath moving light, was not pleased when Don broke the roof tiles of his house, overlooking the ground.

In Buckinghamshire we played in the **Burnham C.C.** Week. For many years we had the honour of the Friday fixture which was always followed by a grand barbecue thrown for the whole village. There the local twins Judy and June worked overtime to entertain the visiting cricketers. On one occasion we introduced into Frost, David Sheppherd, then with Gloucestershire and now a Test Match umpire. He scored seventy or so runs and given the chance to bowl took a few wickets. Our captain asked if he would tell Michael Proctor, his county captain, about his runs. He replied 'No, but I will tell him about the wickets'. **Normandy** had a ground, excavated by the Army from scrubland on the Surrey/Hampshire border. Here we played in their week in July, led by Roger Hunt.

ASSORTED EARLY MATCHES – ALMOST LICQUORICE

Various other assorted games were held in the first fifteen years. A series of games came about under the banner **Jack Frost IInd XI**. We already had a game on the day we were invited to play **Hugh Roach Kelly's Gentlemen of All Ireland** on the Milbourne Lodge School Ground at Claygate. Roach was a master at the school and had very strong connections with London Irish R.F.C. from whence he drew most of his players. These games gave us the opportunity to turn out a team made up of umpires, scorers, cripples, hangers on and Horner. They were great social events as the Irish racked up a barrel of Guinness in the pavilion. On one occasion they included in

III – MID-WEEK FROSTING

their team, Welsh Rugby International and broadcaster, Cliff Morgan. The cricket went well but Frost easily came a poor second in the seven-a-side rugby match which followed.

We also played the odd game or two against **Send Occasionels**, a wandering side raised by musician Anthony Phillips, a founder member of pop group Genesis. These were always fun with lots of interesting characters and lovely girls around.

TRIANGULAR CRICKET

So as to extend the season further we arranged a triangular tournament in mid-October on Hare Lane Green, the Leverets ground. The sides were Jack Frost XI, **Leverets** and **Merton Alcoholics**. Play began at 11am and often lasted into the gloom. The games were played on a Sunday and a licence extension at the Swan enabled everyone to enjoy food and drink all day.

Esher Cricket Club
The spacious New Road Ground of Esher Cricket Club where many Jack Frost XI games were played, including Peter Parfitt's XI, the Madras and Pasadena clubs.

Chapter IV – HOME GAMES

It is quite unusual for a nomadic side to play home fixtures. However, there were occasions when we wished to play cricket against a few of the wandering sides we had come to know. Quite a number of such sides had been formed during the sixties, although sadly many of these have since flounded. **Merton Alcoholics**, I have earlier mentioned, the **Bootleggers**; founded by Peter Marsh, **The Crickets**; from whom we stole Brian Rhodes and **Sons of Bacchus**; put together by Tony Curtis-Evans around a nucleus of **Old Sherbernens**. We had a regular fixture with **Pyrford Cricket Club**, who have a nice ground on Lord Iveagh's estate in Surrey some five miles off the old A3 London to Guildford road. Our association with Pyrford became most friendly and thus they agreed to our making use of their wicket when not in use by themselves. This arrangement continued for some four or five years enabling us to meet other cricket clubs sans grounds. Unfortunately, it was yet another altecation over televised World Cup Association Football that brought this to an end.

After this TV Soccer incident the Jack Frost XI Committee instructed the fixture secretary to write to opponents, for matches due to be played during future Association Football World Cup Tournaments, asking for their assurance that these matches do not be shown in their clubhouses, as it interrupted both play and socialising. We generally beat Pyrford despite their having one very good all-round player, who hit the ball very hard and bowled fiercely fast left arm round the wicket. The demise of this bowler almost came about when on one occasion he was poleaxed with a throat chop by umpire M.P.R.Welch as he signalled a no ball with the wrong arm. The games against the **Bootleggers** are best remembered by the yard-of-ale drinking after the game. Peter Marsh had presented the yard glass as a trophy for our games and was used with much vomiting over the years. **The Sons of Bacchus** are a fine wandering side including some very classy cricketers. Not least of which was Ian F.C.Brown, another Old Citizen, who we soon poached, when not playing for Bacchus. Ian became our Insurance Policy as he invariably took his score over fifty on each and every Frost innings.

Our only chance when playing Bacchus was when Tony Curtis-Evans bowled, which as skipper he did badly and a lot. Sons of Bacchus played a number of two innings matches spread over two days, which nearly saw the end of Mr.Gill when making a guest appearance at the Sherborne School cricket ground and was over the two innings required to bowl 48 overs. On a another occasion they played a two day game against **Teddington C.C.** This game was reduced to one day when Froster, Simon Reed took ten of their first innings wickets for few runs. The Crickets were our opponents at a number of different venues until they merged and played at the ground of **Effingham Cricket Club**. This fixture was discontinued due to both the attitude of their senior and ancient player, Len Gurgelston; or some such name; and the eight

IV – HOME GAMES

o'clock closing of their pavilion bar. On another singular occasion we were running short on extended season games and due to the auspices of original Froster, Tommy Booth, we were able to make use of the Imperial Club ground at Mitcham. Not having an opponent we made use of the Club Cricket Conference Emergency Fixture Bureau.

Much to our surprise and delight we were allocated the strong Surrey club side, **Old Emmanuel**, led by the formidable Derek Newton. Their XI containing the likes of Victor Dodds, and more famous names of that era were far to strong for us, particularly when middle order batsman, Robin Needham scored a very quick half-century. The evening antics proved by far the most interesting when their skipper was overheard to ask I.F.C.Brown why such a good cricketer 'should play for such a rabble?' Brown's reply that he enjoyed playing cricket for Jack Frost XI was not understood. However, the evening extended into great hilarity when Robin Needham introduced us to the numbers game. The outcome of the game being that the losers put some coins into a jug and drank a pint of beer. Not wishing to put hand in pocket, Chris Horner took the game very seriously, with much clicking of fingers and shouting of numbers. Robin castigated Horner, 'The idea of this game is not to win but to loose'. Immediately the numbers game became an integral part of Frost cricket legend and most significantly Robin Needham was recruited to play for Frost. A natural for this great character.

Another Frost feature, much used when the home side appeared to be dwindling from the bar, is the head count. The side with the least players left in the bar would buy drinks for the opposition.

OVERSEAS VISITORS

It has always been the club policy to entertain visiting overseas cricket teams touring England. No more so when we had previously met them on their home territory. Indeed we had a fund to subsidize such matches. A number of kind and friendly clubs lent us their facilities, to meet overseas opponents, including **Esher C.C.**, **Teddington C.C.**, both a number of times, **Leverets**, and **Oxshott** and **Old Emmanuel's Blagdon's Ground**. I believe the first overseas sides we entertained were a Dutch side, **Groningen University**, at the Leveret's ground at Claygate. The match was played, matting on grass, which was the Hollanders usual playing surface, and their quickie had little difficulty in bowling us out.

We played **North of Ireland** at Blagdon's and managed to chalk up a victory before both sides departed for a dissipated tour of the boozers and strip clubs of the Metropolis. Possibly the most prestigious home match was during the 1970 season on a most delightful sunny day at New Road, Esher. We played a **Middlesex XI** in aid of Peter Parfitt's Benefit Fund. Most of the Middlesex Championship side turned out

IV – HOME GAMES

with a few added in the shape of 'Stewpot' and the great Surrey and England batsman, Ken Barrington. Frost turned out the best side possible which included Roger Hunt, a young Laurence Dillamore and various other worthies. A memorable moment came for the Jack Frost XI Captain, when he bowled Eric Russell and faced the prospect of delivering the next ball to Barrington. Setting the field carefully Mr.Gill decided that a ball good enough to deceive Russell should be good enough for Barrington. Gill was right. The ball turned, went through the gap as Barrington played forward, out of his crease. Barrington stranded, Philip Stevenson, keeping wicket, whipped off the bails appealing loudly to the square leg umpire who to the amazement of all shook his head.

Stevenson ran to the umpire protesting strongly, only to be told that the spectators had not come to Esher to see England's greatest batsman get out first ball. Gill determined to get his revenge delivered the next ball, when the England batsman promptly fell into the trap skiing the ball hard and high into the hands of the strategically placed long off, Roy Furness the best fielder in Frost, who promptly spilled the ball to the ground. Mr.Gill gave up bowling to Ken Barrington. Middlesex batsman Sam Black hit a mighty six which smashed the glass front of the Esher pavilion. When Tony Gill came off the field he did learn that the ball had struck the head of his two year old daughter, Emma who was on her way to Kingston Hospital with a piece of glass embedded in her head. All was well as Emma is unharmed and still alive. Jack Frost XI raised a four figure sum for Parfitt's Benefit much made from an auction of cricketana held in the Esher Pavilion after the match. In the late seventies **University of Toronto** came on tour under the leadership of early Froster, Richard Beale, a great designer but wayward fast bowler who had emigrated to Canada.

We played that match on the Oxshott Village Ground. Many early Frosters turned out to re-meet Richard and a grand party was held in the evening at the Bear Inn. For the quality of the cricket. our match against visiting **Madras** must rank high. Esher kindly lent us their ground for this game played on a beautiful June summers day. The Indians were on a serious tour of England and included a number of State players of great skill. There was great excitement from the opposition when they saw Saeed Hattea carry his bag into our changing room. Cry's of "Hattea from Bombay". At this time he was spending English winter's playing cricket for his city of birth. Winning the toss Madras started their innings close to 11am. Whilst Syd kept their runs down and took two wickets before lunch, other bowlers made little impression. Shortly before lunch their captain, Mr. Azhrauddin came to the wicket. After lunch their skipper let loose with a series of perfectly timed drives to score a century in something like forty minutes before, what seemed like, giving up his wicket without playing a shot shortly before 3.15.

The match was played on Derby Day and it was later revealed that he had never

IV - HOME GAMES

seen the race and wished to watch it on the clubhouse television at 3.15. He had decided to get his century first. Despite some good performances by Jack Frost XI players we were beaten by a better side of Indian cricketers. The evening went with a bang only after Lionel Tye had visited the local Indian Take-away and returned with a boot full of curry for one and all. Following the Jack Frost XI Tour of California, we also played **University of California, Pasadena** and **British Columbia** when they toured England, but more of that later.

Over the years Frost played a number of matches against 'F' Troop, a strong casual side playing their games on the old Gloucestershire county ground. Clifton College. the Troop often contained a number of top-class cricketers including Roy Sweatman and when they visited us at Teddington, Chris Broad. Shown on the College Ground is one of their leading batsmen, and also a Froster Andrew Brearley.

Chapter V – EARLY SUNDAY FIXTURES

During the first ten to fifteen years of the XI we added any number of Sunday fixtures, mainly against Surrey and Sussex villages. This was often due to the fact that at that time an increasing number of our members were living on the North Downs of Surrey.

Rudgwick lies on the Horsham to Guildford road. Quite a strong village club playing on a recreation ground with a small pavilion. However, we have had many an even game with this club and still enjoy playing **Rudgwick C.C.** Over the years we recruited more than the odd player from their ranks including Dennis Wise and Barry McGahan. One of the more memorable games was the occasion when we had to scratch round to make-up the side and recruited a couple of hippy characters. Fortunately we had Bob Hurst who took seven of their wickets. Frost wickets fell regularly as Bob held the other end and accumulated runs. When the ninth wicket fell we were still fifty runs short of their total with Hurst still batting and myself approaching the crease. Bob Hurst was presented with the Man of the Match Award, in the Fox Inn, he having scored the fifty runs to win us the match. He commented 'I had to score the runs as there were only a couple of drug addicts and Gill to bat.'

The Fox at Rudgewick is a most delightful hostelry serving Horsham Ale from the barrel and much loved by real-ale enthusiast, Chris Horner. A further attraction was the piano played by an old dear who we gladly joined in the chorus of such old favourites as 'Roll out the Barrel'. In the same area is **Broadbridge Heath & Merryfield** another fixture played on a wicket cut out of the surrounding heathland. This fixture came to an end when they turned the club into an enormous sports complex. Much more to the Frost style was the **Warnham** fixture, introduced by the elegant early Froster, H.Sydney Smith. A good wicket in a country area surrounded by trees. On this ground Sydney scored eighty runs in an innings reminiscent of Felix with the bat. Immaculate creams topped with silk neckerchief were Sydney's trademark as he glided, cut and drove each ball to the boundary.

It was Sydney Smith who also introduced our treasured fixture against the **Royal Household** within the private grounds of Windsor Castle. For over thirty years Jack Frost XI have been privileged to play this game in the most wonderful surroundings of the private park, overshadowed by the ancient home of the Royal Family. Occasional glimpse of the Royals sweeping down the drive past the ground add to the enjoyment, with opportune visits of H.M.Queen Elizabeth II, exercising her corgis, an event, Mr.Gill did fall fowl of the Comptroller of the Queen's Household when he once stepped over the boundary railing to paint a watercolour of the ground and Queen Victoria's Summer House. A bit of talking had to be done on another occasion when Jamie Hudson decided to try and ride a prize winning Royal donkey. The Household were always a good side difficult to beat on their home ground. Despite including Australian Test bowler, David Gilbert we were still unable to beat them. The

V – EARLY SUNDAY FIXTURES

opposition always insisted upon a Beer Boat Race

Up the river at **Whitchurch** we pay our toll at the bridge over the river Thames, generally after a lunch time session in the Swan at Pangbourne, overlooking the weir. Some good games have been played against this most amiable crowd of cricketers, in the past led by Tim Brickhill. From the very beginning wicket-keeper David Cullen has managed this match. David would often supply a wonderful spread of cheeses, pates and the like from his grocery store. The ground is down a rutted lane and is overlooked by a large hill of most pleasant proportions. A small pavilion provides changing space and teas. There are two pubs in the tiny village with after match drinking taking place in the one where their team had not most recently fallen out. A traditional boat race always took place over the white line on the main, and only, road outside. Traffic is stopped and spectators gathered for this annual event. Although we often as not lost the cricket, Frost always win the boat race.

The year we did win the cricket was when Cullen included an Australian, by the name of Steadman. He opened our bowling, at quite a pace, and was soon amongst the wickets. Mr.Gill felt a compliment was due, and congratulated him upon his spell, only to receive the reply "I'm a batsman not a bowler". Sure enough he was a batsman and scored an untroubled half century. Some of our Surrey Hills members had begun to play their Saturday cricket in local villages, hence our introduction to South **Nutfield** and later **Outwood** and **Abinger**. So it came about that we recruited such dedicated Frosters as, present treasurer, Peter Murray, regular umpire Geoff Last; on occasions to be seen standing in German Officer's uniform; and William Lewis. Brian Martin has for some time run the South Nutfield game whilst Geoff Last does the same at Outwood. The penultimate fixture, and now the last, of the season was **Thursley** on the Surrey/Hampshire borders. This was the first match the club allowed Chris Horner to manage, which he both ran very well and guarded aggressively.

We used to drink in a nearby "County Type" pub, used by the local gentry and run by a very rude Pole. Incidents occurred, we were pleased therefore when Thursley built a proper pavilion with bar. They have a strong team and often used to win the Flora Dora Trophy, the knock-out cup for village cricket in Surrey. Through Michael Watson-Smythe, who was now playing a bit of Frost cricket, he gave us a fixture with his club **Thorpe**, Surrey. Much due to Michael including a number of his personal friends into the Thorpe side, the game was great fun and following a drink in their small pavilion he invited all back to his home, The Clock House at Egham. Much Kummel was consumed. None left until the following day. By the following year Michael had purchases a grand manor house, Great Martins at Waltham St. Lawrence in Berkshire. His primary reason for buying the house was his own cricket ground on the front lawn, to say nothing of the Victorian squash court and billiard room.

V - EARLY SUNDAY FIXTURES

The local **Waltham St. Lawrence** club had for many years had permission to play on the ground and Michael agreed that they may continue provided he became captain, fixture secretary and paid for a new pavilion and bar. Hence, Jack Frost XI commenced a series of matches in most delightful surroundings, with many of the games being played in October, in accordance with our raison d'etre. One particular incident of note was when they produced their champion pint of beer drinker. We produced a thin young man to take up the challenge and bets were struck. When Simon Reed had demolished their Champ, in a second, we picked up our winnings, in Scottish £10 notes, and treated the whole of the Frost team to a restaurant meal. On another occasion Mr. Gill persuade one of Michael and Monica's young nieces to show him the stables. Upon the fall of a wicket Gill went out to bat on horseback, handing the reins to the square leg umpire. Michael was furious that his lawn maybe cut-up by horses hooves.

During Royal Ascot week Michael and his beautiful wife Monica entertained large parties of guests at Great Martins and the races. Following the racing a week of evening cricket games were arranged to entertain the guests. Jack Frost XI were regularly invited to play during these weeks and much enjoyed lavish entertainment and food provided by the "Bailywick" and other restaurants owned by Michael Watson-Smythe. Lionel Tye had farming friends in Bucks and he arranged a Sunday fixture with the local village club in **Little Kingshill**. We always meet for a grand luncheon spread and much beer in a local pub. Ian Gould, who was then playing soccer for Arsenal and keeping wicket for Middlesex, played one of his Frost games here. Besides keeping wicket, he took off his pads to bowl and then batted to score more than a century. Gould played one of the most spectacular shots played in the history of the XI. Running down the wicket to their opening bowler, he jumped both feet off the ground, to cut the ball full toss over the Little Kingshill pavilion. I awarded him the Man of the Match Award for hogging the game. Upon downing the treble scotch, he said in true Gould fashion 'XXXX me. What the XXXX was that'.

The villages and club sides Jack Frost XI played in the first fifteen years of the club set the tone for the successful wandering club Frost have become today.

Royal Household, Windsor Castle
The cricket pitch within the private grounds of Windsor Castle.

Intrepid Opening Pair
Frost stalwart's Chris Horner and David Lipop pose at Whitchurch Cricket Club in 1996.

Brad's 70th Birthday
In 1996 Brad Bradley celebrated his birthday playing cricket for Jack Frost XI against the Royal Household at Windsor. Chairman, Laurence Dillamore *(left)* presents a cake to immediate Past Chairman, Brad Bradley.

Chapter VI – CALIFORNIA HERE WE COME

The crowning glory of the early years came in 1975 when Jack Frost XI planned a cricket tour to California. This came about as I was spending a lot of business time in California. When in Los Angeles I often stayed in the family home of my dear friend Bob Beeney in the Hollywood Hills. Bob is originally from Brenchley in Kent and ran a successful realator business then in the Los Angeles area. One evening, seated in Bob's den consuming copious quantities of gin, Bob suggested that Frost toured California. At that time Bob was an active player and administrator in Southern Californian cricket. There and then on the back of a packet of Senior Service we outlined a possible itinerary. Two years later when we did the tour it was scheduled exactly as that original draft. On returning home I put the concept before the committee and in principal it was agreed that, despite the recession, we tour.

Very soon we had set up a tour committee with various members put in charge of different aspects. The work was put in by such as David Willis, arranging travel and hotels, Brad Bradley in charge of sponsorship and Clive Gregg taking care to produce a thirty-six page glossy brochure; including photographs and pen portraits of tourists. We worked out a budget of around £600 a head, to pay for flights, hotels and car hire. Tourists were asked to pay a monthly standing order to meet their basic cost and a Sponsorship Fund was started to pay for extras, such as fuel, presentations, entertaining, kitty and all those incidentals which can dig into the pocket, Roy Furness set up a trust with Kim Morell and Lionel Citroen joining as trustees to look after the finances. Brad and others did a marvellous job raising sponsorship which in the event totalled some £2,500 in cash plus a large amount of cricket gear, several bats, pads, gloves etc., donated by Gunn & Moore, Red Barrel beer from Watney and cases of Peter Dawson Whisky.

Tour flag, ties and sweaters were specially designed and manufactured. The rule being that only Jack Frost sweaters be worn on the field of play and only club caps when in the field. Much liaison was ongoing with Bob Beeney in L.A. and many social and other arrangements were put in hand on the West Coast. On Maundy Thursday 1975, the Jack Frost XI - Tour of California party, some thirty-one persons met at the Post House Hotel, Gatwick. Through the auspices of David Willis, Trust House Forte provided a farewell reception for Frost. It was March and the weather was diabolical with snow falling heavily with freezing temperatures. It was then that Alan Miller began his antics. He had, immediately prior to the tour broken his arm in a Skiing accident in St. Moritz. Although unable to play, he decided to come for the ride. Looking out of the hotel window at the snow, Miller told everyone that our charter had been cancelled, due to ice on the wings, and we would have to stay the night in the hotel. This had the effect of throwing many into a panic, whilst he and I enjoyed an extended reception, until tourists realised that outside, planes were continually taking off and landing.

VI - CALIFORNIA HERE WE COME

The japes continued when we reached Gatwick Airport Concourse. The P.A. system broadcast, asking Mr. Fred Karno and his army to report to the B.A. desk. The flight over, in the main uneventful, we arrived some thirteen hours later in brilliant sunshine, temperatures in the 90's. The Los Angeles Customs Hall was the scene of the next incident. We had put all the cricket gear into a large painted wooden Victorian Cricket Box, provided by Miller. Mr.Gill had with him a suit of armour destined for a client in L.A. which had been placed under the bats, pads etc. U.S.Customs officers were curious about the big box with the strange sports equipment, so a diversion became necessary. We took out some of the kit and handing a bat to a customs officer proceeded to bowl to him in the customs hall, whist he tried, unsuccessfully, to play off breaks from a baseball stance. U.S.Customs gave up and let us through kit, armour and all. Representatives of Californian cricket,Bob Beeney, John Reid and Leo Magnus were there to greet us with T-Shirts stencilled with our tour logo and individual names sown into the chest.

After a very tired group of Frosters had checked into the Holiday Inn, Westwood, Los Angeles, California, we were greeted by Jack Froster, Lynn Myers who had flown in direct from Australia. Lynn had played a deal of Frost games in the late sixties before returning home to become Deputy Ombudsman for South Australia. He had played his cricket in England for Teddington and was a quite sharp opening bowler, lacking somewhat in the field. Lynn had agreed to share the allocation of the hire cars, with Alan Hawtin. We had hired some dozen cars to allow two to three persons to a vehicle. The day after our arrival a fleet of cars were delivered to the hotel. Miller further confused matters by commandeering a very plush private limousine outside the hotel entrance and telling our cricketers to throw their bags in the trunk. When the very surprised chauffeur returned with his boss he wondered what all the strange bags, bats and assorted Englishers were doing in his luxury vehicle. A day after having left London in a snow storm we were ready to play our first game, a warm up, **Robert Walter Beeney's Heavyweight XI**, in a temperature nearing 100degrees fahrenheit.

The game took place at the Sir C.Aubrey-Smith Field in Griffith Park, Los Angeles. Next to the Cricket Ground was a Mexican Restaurant where Bob treated us to lunch and welcomed us to California before weighing in his team, all of whom tipped the scales at over 200lbs. We found that playing against us was the former captain of **Ringwood C.C.**, Paul Ravera who had by then moved to live in California. We were in the field when our breakthrough came. Star Barbadian batsman and one of the biggest ever hitters in cricket, Donald Weeks glanced a ball to the fine leg boundary where Lynn Myers pounced upon it and hurled the wicket down, thus running him out for a duck. Tired and weary Frosters were revived by an amazing tea break made up of mountains of fresh fruit and home made lemonade. The result of this was that

VI - CALIFORNIA HERE WE COME

we won our first game on tour. Spirits revived we had a wonderful booze up in the adjacent bar with our new found American friends. Next day we met **The Cricket Club of British Columbia** who had come down from Vancouver to tour Los Angeles.

The Canadians had a pair of opening bowlers, both of whom had formerly played in the Lancashire League and certainly knew how to use the ball. However, our batsmen ensured we chalked up an international win on American soil. Day three saw us play **Hollywood Cricket Club** led by an over-the-top Englishman who had the Rolls-Royce franchise for Southern California. He later became Ian Botham's agent and unsucessfully tried to make him the next James Bond. Hollywood Cricket Club mirrors the birth and expansion of the film industry. The burgeoning art form of film attracted a number of British actors to the bright sunlight of America's West Coast, in the period between the wars. The cricket club was founded in 1932 by that great British character actor Sir.C.Aubrey Smith, who had earlier toured South Africa with the Marylebone Cricket Club. P.G. Wodehouse wrote the minutes at the first meeting. Stories abound of the antics of such players as David Niven, Errol Flynn and Boris Karloff. However, their captain on our day did not conduct himself in the spirit of the game, but we did win.

All our games were played on difficult wickets. The American sides usually played matting on grass, but in deference to an English side visiting from 6,000 miles away they had decided to play on grass. The problem with this was that it is customary on the West Coast to sow both summer and winter grass. At the Spring time of our visit the winter grass was dying off and the summer grass just sprouting. This created an uneven surface which, whilst giving our bowlers much help, made batting something of a lottery. Andrew Brearley, arguably our best bat, only lost his wicket, during the tour, by catches off his gloves or handle of the bat. Several dogged batsmen in the middle order, such as Brad Bradley and Clive Gregg worked hard to score our runs. However, our strike bowlers, in particular Miles Pratt and Chris Messenger; bowling left arm quick; together with Lynn Myers, posed problems for our opposition.

With a playing party of some twenty-four members, the others being wives and girlfriends, the selection committee of Brad, Dandridge and Gill had to balance the Frost sides, whilst giving those who wanted, at least five games out of the twelve scheduled. At this stage our toughest opponents were **University of California Los Angeles**. This side was made up of students and lecturers at one of the largest universities in the world. They attracted students from afar including many West Indian, Indian, English and antipodeans. Many were good cricketers, including run machine, Donald Weeks; who held a certificate from President Nixon recognising him as the greatest all-round sportsman in the U.S.A. David Dandridge skippered Frost in a very hard fought game which we narrowly won. We were cock-a- hoop at this

VI - CALIFORNIA HERE WE COME

feather in our cap. **The Southern Californian Cricket Association** and their associated clubs gave us a great deal of hospitality, following most of the games and we were pleased to have the sponsorship fund under our belt so as to respond.

The President of the SCCA was a delightful Oriental American, by the name of Gene Wong, who seemed to own a large number of department stores and was mad on cricket. He hosted a lavish party for Jack Frost XI at his sumptuous home where we added to the fare by providing the Red Barrel, kindly delivered to us by Watney's. Many other parties, official and ad hoc, were thrown by our hosts throughout the tour and quite a few friendships, male and female, were made over the three weeks we were in their country. 'My, you have a wonderful English accent, Gee'. This phrase often issued from the mouths of blonde, freckled, retrousse nosed, young California girls. One of the strangest parties we attended was at the opulent home in Pacific Palisades of a banking friend of the Citroen brothers. Ossie Goran was our host and he went to extraordinary lengths to show off his wealth. We were all forced to take part in a series of house tours conducted by his wife. It was rather as if we were visitors to a stately home except here money took the place of style. At various points of the evening Ossie did not flinch from giving us the running total, to the nearest Grand, how much the do was costing him.

On the way to the exclusive enclave housing Ossie's estate, together with Lionel Tye, I was in the car driven by Michael Citoen. As we sought our destination, Michael commented he, 'Was not sure where his friend Ossie lived'. Lionel replied, 'I know where all my friends live'. A grand and wonderful evening was had in the ostentatious home of Ossie Goran. After about seven or eight days we set off in our hire-cars for the Northern Californian part of the tour, and arrived safely despite the driving of Brad and Kim, before having to return for several important games in the South. Our first stop was at **Santa Barbara** where we played on a school ground, surrounded by palm trees. and perched on a cliff edge overlooking the ocean. It must be one of the most beautiful cricket grounds in the world. The weather was wonderful and the temperature in the 100's. Brad Bradley, who captained this game for Frost, and Miles Pratt had the unenviable job of opening the bowling in the great heat. As we had been told that Santa Barbara Cricket Club was not very strong we had made room for some of our weaker tourists.

Unfortunately there was a distinct lack of Frost bowlers, necessitating the openers to bowl the greater part of their innings. Their batting had been strengthened by two Jamaicans, enlisted for the day from the Los Angeles League, who went on to score a lot of runs. Fortunately on a good wicket our batters were in form and we managed to save the day. An unusual part of the post match celebrations was the English fish and chip shop, in which we were entertained. Unlike at home it provided large jugs of

VI - CALIFORNIA HERE WE COME

beer. The trip on towards San Francisco gave us the opportunity to travel one of Americas most scenic drives, along the Big Sur, skirting the Pacific Ocean most of the way. After a sight seeing stop to visit the outrageous Madonna Inn at San Luis Obispo and a look over the hedge of W.Randolph Hearst's San Simeon mansion we passed through Carmel to stay overnight at Monterey. Here some of the party dined on Fisherman's Wharf, made famous by John Steinbeck, with first class fish cuisine, view over the famous Monterey Bay and seabed floodlighting alongside the wharf.

The following day we made our way into San Francisco and checked into the Holiday Inn which is in the centre of Chinatown. Besides the two scheduled games, **San Jose** and **Marin County** we had allowed a few free days to allow the tour party to do there own thing whilst in this exciting city. Whilst a few, Gerry Collis, Andrew Brearley and David Dandridge, headed off showgirl seeking in Las Vegas, Robin Sculthorpe and others to Death Valley, we later wished that party had not returned, (Whatever happened to the Jack Frost Tour film, Robin?). Others found the showing of Deep Throat at the local movie house quite tempting. More found the Golden Gate Tennis Club, Racquets Club, Thomas Lord's Restaurant; complete with menus on cricket bats, The Vintner Wine Bar, oriental exercises and food to our taste. It was whilst we were in the city that prime joker Alan Miller got his just desserts. A lady lawyer friend of mine had telephoned to arrange for her and I to dine together. Miller, with whom I shared a room, took the call and told her I had been arrested for drunk driving. A very serious offence in California.

The lady immediately used her legal skills to find where I was held, without success, of course. When the lady and I dined she enquired about my brush with the law, to which I was oblivious. She was furious about this Miller scam and took her revenge. The following day she made an arrangement with 'Dial-a-Pie' for a 'Custard Pie' to be delivered into Miller's face in the main lobby of the hotel. He had to see the funny side of it as with much amusement Frosters watched him wipe the remains off his body and clothes. It was again at this hotel when I was awoken, in the early hours, by hammering on the door. Slumped against the door post was the bedraggled form of Alan Miller, supported by a large hotel security man. The Hotel Detective needed assurance that the figure he was escorting was in fact my room mate before making me sign a receipt for him and pushing Miller into my arms. The game against San Jose proved the most disappointing. This city is industrial and can best be compared to Slough on a wet Winter's day. It was mostly populated by blue collar workers, many of them expatriate British from Birmingham and Newcastle, even having it's own Working-man's Club.

Played on a wet day on a playing field overshadowed by an industrial plant, our hearts were not in the game. However, we fought another victory. Following the match

VI – CALIFORNIA HERE WE COME

we adjourned to the Anglo-American club. For our benefit, as they were sure we craved for English food, they had laid on a bangers and mash supper. However, the bonus was the wine laid on by their patron, wine grower Paul Masson who provided several cases of his prime vintage Cabinet Sauvignon. After 'Supper' we were required to sing for it. Frosters on tour do not know the words to many clean songs and after Miller had done a solo recounting the nocturnal antics of his sister in gay Pariee, the San Jose players wives showed some discontent. The embarrassing situation was overcome by Lynn Myers, leading in a lusty rendition of 'Waltzing Matilda' which pleased them more. Crossing the Golden Gate Bridge to play Marin County was in contrast a sheer delight. The Marin ground is rather like an English village ground, but more so with, during our game, a deer picking its way down a wooded hillside before crossing the field of play.

The Marin County side were the leaders of the Northern Californian League and included the three Sarapachi brothers who hailed from Sri Lanka and had been coached at good cricket schools on the island. Marin batted strongly, building a high score, when much to our surprise the umpires lifted the bails and the batsmen walked off. We assumed that they had declared for an early tea, only to learn that, they being use to limited overs games, had taken up their allocated overs. Mr.Gill protested that there had been no mention of it being a limited over game and Jack Frost XI never play this bastardized form of the game. Marin's captain Ken Sarapachi agreed to play normal hours with a finish at 6pm. They elected to bat on after tea, amassing a big score and leaving us just about an hour to get them. Frost batted out a draw. Whilst in San Francisco, though the good auspices of Bob Beeney who made it possible, there was the opportunity for the keen golfers to play some of the best courses in the World. Located on the Carmel Peninsular are three Championship Course of World renown where, on two, our tourists were able to play.

Together with **Palm Springs**, played earlier on the tour, **Pebble Beach** and **Cyprus Point** were played thus adding up to three of the four championship courses, West of the Rockies. The San Francisco part of the Californian Tour was probably the time most enjoyed time by Frosters. However we still had much cricket and socialising to come and the party flew back to Los Angeles to resume residence at the Westwood Holiday Inn.

THE MINI-TEST MATCH

Our first object was to prepare for the big match, which was against the **Combined Southern Californian Cricket Association XI**, who selected from sixteen clubs with a total of 32 sides. The Mini-Test loomed and it was decided that our selection committee should meet with the cricket gurus of the SCCA, former Indian Test player,

VI - CALIFORNIA HERE WE COME

Lashkari and former Lancashire County professional John Reid, so that we may get some idea of the opposition strength. Lashkari explained that their batting, whilst strong, may be tested by our opening attack, Chris Messenger's left arm deliveries being feared in particular. We met and selected what we considered to be the best side available and the next day presented ourselves and fellow tourists at the Sir C. Aubrey Smith Field, Griffith Park, Los Angeles, U.S.A.

As all our matches in California had been well covered in the Los Angeles press, we had built up quite a following of supporters who turned out at Griffith Park for this major match. Knowing of their respect for our opening bowlers, I won the toss and put them in. Certain Frost tourists (Dandridge) have not, even to this day, forgiven me for this decision. I was sure that Miles Pratt and Chris Messenger in particular would be difficult to get away on the sporting track. Wrong. I was not aware of the fact that Chris Messenger was no where to be found. He was in Mexico City becoming engaged to a Grand Young Lady of Old Mexico. The Southern Californian's soon piled on the runs with Donald Weeks and their captain Oscar Durity, who had in the West Indies only a couple of months earlier taken a century and double century, in the same match, from the Australian tourists, uncontained by our bowlers. Enough is to say that we were thoroughly beaten, in fact the only game we lost on that tour.

I was somewhat fazed when, awaiting with some dread my turn to bat, a Los Angles Black and White sirened across the ground and pulled up with a screech of tyres and cloud of dust, as only police can do whilst about their lawful business, outside the pavilion. Never the less I feared these unsolicited visitors less than I feared loosing the big match. Out rushed two of Los Angeles finest and enquired if I were Tony Gill. They explained that the Los Angeles Police Department Chief, Mr. Ed Davies had sent them with the most urgent message from No.10, Downing Street requesting me to immediately telephone the Prime Minister. Realising that it was, of course, some sort of skam, I promised the concerned fuzz that I would call as soon as I had completed my innings, which would not be very long. Nor was it. When I arrived back at the Holiday Inn, the manager rushed across to me and asked if I had called the Prime Minister. I assured him I had. Peter Grainger and David Willis had been put in charge of arranging, for all our tour opponents, the match Jack Frost XI Party.

They had taken a suite in the hotel and layed on piles of food, bottles of booze and music. They had made a pyramid of the bottles of Peter Dawson Whisky, in front of which press photographs were taken, resulting in the distillers later offering to sponsor any future Frost tours. The Californian's were most impressed by our reception and said it was the best 'Thank You' they had ever been given, including MCC and several counties. Most of the teams with whom we had fixtures were welcomed at a the first class party. Pennants and plaques (Where is the S.C.C.A. plaque now?) were

VI – CALIFORNIA HERE WE COME

exchanged and speeches made. I had the unenviable task of presenting a tour tie to the SCCA Captain, Oscar Durity. With the music and drinking in full swing Gill was called to the telephone to take a call from the Chief of Police. A young lady biting my ear and loud background music, to say nothing of the bottle of Dawsons Whisky in one hand did not help in my taking this call.

Mr. Ed Davis enquired 'Had I spoken to Prime Minister James Callaghan?' It was somewhat difficult explaining that I had indeed and lying, added that I would ensure that his diligent action would be reported to Washington when I arrived there next day. He thanked me much and I hung up much relieved. You are not, without thinking, voluntarily economical with the truth to American City Police Chiefs. It was not until we returned home that our suspicions on the origin of this scam were confirmed. From his Surrey home, Michael Welch had planned and performed the telephone freak by ringing, at his home, the American Ambassador to the Court of St. James to enquire the score. Furious that the representative of the United States Government was not aware of the result, he was referred to the L.A. police chief. This bit of nonsense did earn Michael a home visit from Scotland Yard's Special Branch.

Pasadena Cricket Club, one of the most thriving clubs in the area was the Pasadena Cricket Club, led by our old friend from Ringwood, Paul Ravera. Despite John Isaacs leadership, we managed to beat Pasedena on a hot sticky day.

HER MAJESTY'S CONSULATE-GENERAL For our penultimate game, Jack Frost XI had the privilege of playing the opening match on the newly purpose-built Los Angeles Civic Cricket Stadium. For this prestigious game, which attracted a deal of publicity throughout California, our opponents were the British Consular-General's XI led by the Consular-General himself. The side was made-up of Diplomatic Corps worthies with a number of selected local cricketing stars. The match was played on the new wicket which lacked much life but was at least flat. In a low scoring game, we again managed to finish victorious. We had a further honour when, together with officials of the Southern Californian Cricket Association, we were invited to an evening official reception at the Residence of the Consular- General. The SCCA explained that such an honour as this had not been extended to a visiting English team for over a decade, after a visit by Yorkshire C.C.C. when a Mr.Frederick Sewell Trueman had an incident involving the Consular-General's daughter, a waiter and the swimming pool.

We were advised to be on our best behaviour and respect the diplomatic niceties. However, there was no allowing for Alan Miller who when departing, thanked H.M.C.G. for a most sumptuous reception and said he would be having a word with the Foreign Secretary to tell him how the Consulate was wasting British tax-payers

VI - CALIFORNIA HERE WE COME

money. The most delightful diplomat was, of course, not fazed by Mr.Miller. This followed an earlier embarrassment when, in a loud voice, Miller offered 'a dime for the old trout in the corner', whereupon a senior official of the SCCA protested that she was his wife. In many places we went we were served with English food, in the mistaken assumption that we had travelled 6,000 miles to the land of plenty to enjoy what we normally eat at home. This reception was no exception. It was indeed a lavish affair and Frosters, in the main, behaved by keeping away from young girls and the swimming pool.

The final fixture was scheduled against **Dr.Clifford Severn's XI**. The good doctor was a dietician much consulted by Hollywood movie stars and Olympic athletes. He was a genuine English eccentric of indeterminable age, although we celebrated his eightieth birthday on the day of the Consulate- General's game. He had come to Hollywood between the wars to make films and more than a dollar or two. He was exceedingly fit and during his visits to our games insisted on walking on his hands around the outfield. Dr. Severn also claimed to be, at 70 years plus, the oldest man to have played cricket at Lord's. He had two sons, reasonable cricketers, who had played against us in earlier games. Most unfortunately, the last match of the tour, against Dr.Clifford Severn's XI had to be cancelled due to a tropical storm which swept Southern California.

CLOSING CALIFORNIAN THOUGHTS During the three weeks of the tour many escapades took place and much fun was had by one and all. I will never forget Alan Hawtin's face when he realised that he was responsible for explaining to Avis Car Rentals that the Jack Frost XI Captain had left his hire car in Dean Martin's swimming pool. The reactions of the tourists, when they were incorrectly advised that a traffic jam on the Big Sur was due to Kim Morell ploughing his car into a deep ravine, were quite revealing. Alan Miller had been to work when Brad became most upset at a phone call from his wife Peggy, back at home. The excitement on our floor of the Holiday Inn when Alan Miller and Mr. Gill forcefully ejected an uninvited pimp and two hookers from their room. Someone else had laid on a scam.

The perpetrators of the skam on David Dandridge are known. After one match David complained of a migraine and begged his leave to return to the hotel. However, before leaving he was most anxious to convert sterling cash into dollars. This made Gerry Collis and Andrew Brearley suspicious as to why he should need an amount of local currency when he was returning to bed. With the connivance of Egypt, the cocktail waitress at the hotel, they ascertained that Dandridge had probably ordered a hooker for 10pm. Whereupon, they got onto the blower and set about ordering a stream of different girls to come to Dandridge's room at that exact time. At ten o'clock they sat in the entrance of the cocktail bar looking out onto the lobby watching some

VI - CALIFORNIA HERE WE COME

ten or twelve ladies of the street going into the lift and quickly coming back down. We never discovered what did happen in David's hotel room. Towards the end of the tour, The President of the Southern Californian Cricket Association, Gene Wong, invited me to lunch and asked if the were an improvements to their way of cricket, that I may suggest.

I recommended that they cease using the Kookaburra balls that were prevalent out there. These balls of Australian manufacture were very hard and tended to break bats. I also advised that they did not play any more matches without matting. Jack Frost XI later had the pleasure of presenting all our Gunn & Moore equipment to the SCCA for the benefit of local young cricketers.

Homeward Unbound The return flight was not without incident. Fearing the worst of British Airways bar stocking, for a very long flight, we had taken the precaution of buying a number of extra bottles of gin to take with us on the flight. Prior to departure, bumping into the Chief Steward, Gill bet him $50 that the plane would run out of gin before arrival at Gatwick. Sure enough, halfway across the Atlantic the cabin staff announced that all the gin had been consumed. At this Frosters produced a dozen bottles of gin and procuring jugs of ice and tonic water, from the galley, served all the jumbo passengers with complimentary gin and tonic from the Jack Frost XI Californian Cricket Tour party.

Most passengers were delighted until one stuffy gent complained that English sportsmen should be better behaved. He was soon put down by an American lady passenger who told him she had watched us play cricket in Los Angeles and we were all good guys. The B.A.Steward, Mr. McGregor did not pay his bet.

The Jack Frost XI tour to California was the most successful enterprise undertaken by the club and did a great deal to spread our popularity not only in the U.S.A. but in English cricket circles.

Leaving for California March 1975
Brad Bradley, David Willis and Brian Cox are preparing to leave for Gatwick Airport on 27th March, 1975. 24 hours later they were playing cricket under a blazing sun at Griffith Park, Los Angeles.

Chapter VII – 1975 AND ONWARD

Apart from the Jack Frost XI Tour of California, over March and April, the year 1975 saw Frost establish a new cricketing record, fitting for its title. Jack Frost XI played cricket in England every calendar month of the year. The record was submitted, by Bill Frindall, to the Guinness Book of Records but was rejected on the grounds that in future it could be equalled and thus was not a unique record. Some ten years earlier we had started playing matches on Boxing Day at such venues as Surbiton Hockey Club, summer home ground of **Ditton Hill C.C.**, and later at **Teddington C.C.** in Bushy Park. These were treated very much as fun games and we usually managed to include a couple or more of delightful young ladies to dress and field in the slips, which acted as much encouragement to draw players from cold turkey, their wives, children, grannies and mothers-in-law at home. The Danford family, Geoffrey, Gene and their girls usually, after the game, provided a slap up lunch of hot food whilst Michael Welch provided drumsticks of quail, the size of matchsticks.

In the afternoon we would repair to the Swan at Claygate to continue the Yuletide celebrations. This came to an abrupt end when Welch referred to landlord, Len King, as Len Profit and accused him of rooking us. We were all asked to leave. Our revenge came when all the furniture from the Swan Inn dining room was removed into the back of Johnny Mumford's van and installed in the bar of the Wheatsheaf on the Green at Esher, where the party continued, under the eye of the new licensee thankful for his new furniture. The New Year's Day games were well established and the regular fixture list covered the summer months and April and October. This left February, March and November for us to arrange matches. One of these was against **Bill Frindall's XI** played at **Westcott Cricket Club** in February 1975. Bill had played a few Frost games and even showered manege a trois over a New Year weekend, in the New Forest. We were able to include mostly those members and probationers who would be touring California the following month.

Two other matches were fitted into the calendar so as to set our record. The March game was against **Reigate Pilgrims**, who were in many respects the Sunday side of **Reigate Priory**, then one of our regular fixtures.

NEW REGIME

Following the Jack Frost XI Tour of California, Tony Gill relinquished his overall position in the club and left the running of the club completely in the hands of the committee. It had been tacitly agreed that the California Tour had been so good that it should not be recreated, at least for some time. Nor was it repeated. The committee under the main influence of Chris Horner, Richard Davey and Norman Gray considered the next tour. Jack Frost had an unusual Hon. Secretary at that time. Lynn Davey was a rare female cricket club officer. Lynn did a first class job for a couple of years or more.

VII – 1975 AND ONWARD

The first Cricket World Cup was held in England in 1975. Amongst those taking part was a team representing East Africa. An integral member of this side was Harry Shah from Kenya. During his stay Harry played a few games for **Indian Gymkhana** where we came across him when we had a fixture with that club in West London. Very soon he was much enjoying playing for Jack Frost XI. Harry Shah was impressed that we had just completed a tour of California, a very rare event in those days, and suggested that we take a side to **Kenya**. Harry was back in England recently in his capacity as Manager of Kenya in the 1999 World Cup. The committee gave a deal of consideration to this suggestion and, realising that cricket in that country was very strong, decided that provided we could engage our very best players a tour should be undertaken. Thus the tour party would be selected and invitations were sent out to our better players, with mixed results.

TOURING KENT

As during 1975 I was living with Roger Day in Marden and playing my cricket for the village, a decision was made to undertake a Jack Frost XI tour to that area. The committee decided that the tour party to Kent should be made up of only those members invited to tour Kenya. A number of fixtures were undertaken over the later part of a week, the first of these against a small but strong club, **Castle Hill**. Frost put on a good show with Robin Crawford our main wicket taker and run scorer. On the Friday we played **Mote Cricket Club** on the County Ground in Mote Park, Maidstone. Despite a spirited attack by Richard Davey and Brad Bradley, who had previously opened the bowling against the Mote before the war, we made little impression on their batting, missing Robin Crawford's leg-spin, he having gone AWOL, a lady was involved. With former Kent opening bowlers, Sayer and Page, against us we did not put up much resistance and lost heavily.

The Saturday saw us playing on Day Field against **Marden Cricket Club**, who laid on a riotous party in their pavilion. This tour resulted in the Frost committee realising that without the input of our best cricketers, who were in the main not available, Jack Frost XI would not have the strength to mount a decent tour of Kenya. The next year we followed up our visit to Marden by undertaking a cricketing weekend, open to all our members and their ladies. The concept was that we should play Marden in two separate matches on the Saturday and the Sunday, and just as importantly have a great party weekend with one of the most sociable village cricket clubs in Kent, if not England. Indeed we achieved this. Marden are certainly not country bumpkins and had then recently reached the semi-final of the Village Knock Out Cup. They included some class cricketers, as could be seen by the Eton Ramblers caps, MCC sweaters and the like worn by their side.

VII - 1975 AND ONWARD

The weather was glorious and on the Saturday we lost the toss and Marden batted with Doug Worley, who regularly scored a thousand runs a year and by the time we played was well on the way to 2000, opening. We opened the attack with a young Stephen Bartley, an all-rounder who had represented Old Wykehamists in the winning Cricketer Cup team. The first ball of the game, Stephen bowled a fast inducker which comprehensibly bowled Worley neck and crop. We went on to win that game without trouble. The girls joined in great celebrations in and outside the Marden Pavilion with much champagne being consumed. The following morning Marden's Gerald Tomkinson and Roger Day decided, prior to the game, to sabotage Frost by inviting us to a picnic in a wood and serving copious quantities of devastatingly potent locally made cider. Further disruption came about by Captain of the Day, Brian Martin deciding to drop Michael Copleston from the game in favour of former German spy, Gunter Schultz. Michael had shown some peevishness at not opening the bowling the previous day. He took his wife and his car and went home.

The Sunday game started with Stephen Bartley repeating the same first ball to Doug Worley with the same result. Marden no runs for one wicket. Doug Worley was not best pleased. However Marden did go on to beat us, so honours were equal over the weekend.

WILTSHIRE TOURS

The next move was to make our first tour to Wiltshire. Under the stewardship of Chris Horner we played three games over a long weekend. The village of **Poulshott** have a typical Wiltshire country cricket pitch on open land on the edge of a sprinkling of buildings. **Keevil** is a very different kettle of fish, with the wicket set in a semi-bowl within the grounds of Keevil Manor. Delightful hospitality was proffered by the owners of the historic home, with a tasty country tea of scones, butter, jam and cream served in the rose garden. Due to the geographical location, none too distant from Bristol, a number of Jack Frost XI West Country members would play in the tour matches. Tony Heath and P.J.Probyn were regular players on this delightful country tour.

A further element was the inclusion, on at least one occasion, of a number of Australians touring in England with the **Manly Warratahs**. For some years Frost had a one off fixture against the strong club of Cirencester in Gloucestershire which, besides an element driving down from closer to London, in the main our players were drawn from our strong membership in the West Country. **Cirencester Cricket Club** have a large and well manicured ground near the centre of the town, on the edge of the Cotswolds, and is much respected as an important cricket venue. Another fixture of interest around this time was our being invited to play a match at **Henley Cricket Club**

VII - 1975 AND ONWARD

for the inauguration of their new pavilion. The game was played, with a display of mighty hitting from Don Weeks, followed by the opening ceremony conducted jointly by the Frost President and Stuart Story. Much draft Henly Ale was provided and consumed. Around this time a one off weekend tour took place to **Dunfermline** organised by Bill Lewis.

THE YANKS WERE COMING
We were pleased to entertain our friends from North America who toured England over the next couple of years. We played **U.C.L.A.**, **British Columbia** and **Pasadena** on their tours. Teddington Cricket Club hosted our game against British Columbia, who brought a strong side with a couple of American club players added. We were on the wrong side of a win when two of their guest players dug in, after lunch, and accumulated runs. A diversion was called for. Without consultation Alan Miller and Mr. Gill, spotting a passing helicopter, discussed the imminent arrival of our monarch. This was sufficient to break the concentration of the stubborn pair. It was explained to them that as British Columbia were the first Commonwealth side to play cricket in a Royal Park, H.M.Queen Elizabeth II would at tea time be dropping in to meet the teams. As Frosters scoffed sandwiches and cakes the B.C. players drew themselves up outside the pavilion wearing blazers and ties. The Queen did not arrive, nor did we win the game.

Pasadena brought over a great number of the friends we had met on our tour, including our old friend from Ringwood, Paul Ravera who captained their side. We played them on the New Road Ground of **Esher Cricket Club**. They were not very strong but never the less they ran us to the wire. Come the last over they required two runs to win with skipper, Ravera facing at the crease. Mr. Gill faced his responsibility and did the honourable thing by taking the ball for the captain to captain challenge. Gill bowled five dot balls before, with the last ball of the match bowling the Pasadenian through the gate. The proudest ball Mr. Gill ever bowled resulted in a Jack Frost XI victory. A vast gallonage of champagne followed, making the post match celebrations one of the best in Frost annals.

WISDEN AND OTHER PUBLICATIONS
That year, 1976 Jack Frost XI got a mention in Wisden Cricketers' Almanack recording our tour of California the previous year.

In the late seventies Pavilion Books published two anthologies on cricket in strange locations. 'Far Pavilions' and 'Further Pavilions', Edited by Leo Cooper, they include contributions by Tony Gill on Jack Frost XI touring in Ireland and California.

In the early eighties Jack Frost XI, through the auspices of the Stephen Bartley

VII - 1975 AND ONWARD

Gallery, commissioned an oil painting of their matches against the Leverets on Hare Lane Green, Claygate, Surrey. Arist of great repute, Liz Wright, conducted a lot of research before producing an excellent image of our games, depicting many members on the field of play. Unfortunately, the artist sold the painting overseas, but not before one hundred signed and numbered prints were produced and framed in maple, for sale to the members. (Should anyone know the whereabouts of print 'Number One', please tell Mr.Gill as it belongs to him.)

The painting is reproduced on the cover of this book, with much thanks to the artist, LizWright, who gave her permission.

California Tour Team 1975
Prior to off, the tour party played a number of warm-up matches. Shown is the team at Teddington C.C.

VII – 1975 AND ONWARD

Meeting of Cricket Brains
Tony Gill (left) discusses the game with Simon Day, the Chairman of Marden Cricket Club, Kent, in the Marden Club House.

Jack Frost XI Golf
Lunch is much a part of Frost golf matches, as maybe gathered from this picture taken at Effingham Golf Club in 1989.

Chapter VIII – FUNCTIONS OF FUN

Prior to Jack Frost XI's eighth season, in 1968 we organised our first Annual Dinner. Two old Rutlishians, David Willis and Michael Copleston put the function together at the **Worcester Rooms**, Surrey. There was a turn-out of some one hundred members and guests, many from the clubs who by then we were playing on a regular basis. On this first occasion, whilst I spoke; and did so for the next five years; **Babs Clarke** proposed the guests, with what was probably the worst after dinner speech ever and anywhere. The following speaker was the great **Robin Needham**, one of the best after dinner speakers, ever and everywhere. Our Guest of Honour, we had brought up **Cyril Browning**, the landlord of The Star Inn, Ringwood who entertained well. It is a tradition with Jack Frost XI that we never pay our speakers so the list does much credit to the club, all doing the task for their own enjoyment.

After but a few years the Dinner had built a reputation as a good night out for cricketers, from near and far. Many guests came for the fun of it, not just to speak. One year we had eleven county cricketers, two of whom had played for England, whilst the host of BBC Grandstand, **Frank Bough**, was a guest and gave us a mention on TV the following Saturday. Whilst keeping faith with our old friends, **Peter Cooper** from New Milton, **Tommy Booth** and **Jimmy O'Connor**; Leverets there were from Kent **Roger Day**, **Gerald Tomkinson** and **John Burley**; who flew in from Guernsey just to speak. We had also had a number of names, some famous, speak at the Worcester Rooms in the sixties and early seventies. **Ken Barrington in 1972, C.C.W.Box-Grainger President of the Cricket Society in 1970**; he returned to speak 24 years later at the R.A.C.; **Neil Durden-Smith in 1977 and '87, Arnold Long, Surrey, Peter Parfitt 1969 and Alec Bedser**, when Chairman of Selectors, had a bread roll reception, were all Guest Speakers at the Worcester Rooms.

By the late seventies we moved the venue to the **Turk's Head in Twickenham**, but continued to keep the function in the same vain. Speakers there included **Cardew Robinson in 1978** and the following year, England bowler **Jack Young** spoke of his battles with Don Bradman in 1948. Also that year character actor, **Sam Kydd** recounted how, when he was a prisoner of war, they played Test Matches, England v Australia with the German camp guards acting as umpires. A host of top cricketers attended our special 21st Dinner at Church House, Westminster in 1982. Guests included **Michael Procter, Ken and David Graveney** whilst **David Green** made the guest speech. Frost speakers were **Kim Morell, Robin Needham** and myself. Two hundred Frosters and guests attended and for the first and only time ladies were invited. Chris Clayton was arrested outside the portals of Westminster Palace wearing a ladies coat (Viv's) he had mistakenly taken from a cloakroom peg. It has always been a tradition at Jack Frost XI dinners that the loyal toast is given at the beginning of the meal. This allows the President to smoke between courses.

VIII - FUNCTIONS OF FUN

It came to light, some three years later, that the caterers for Church House had gone into liquidation without invoicing Jack Frost XI for the Dinner. We agreed a settlement with the liquidator on very good terms. Thus the most ambitious and expensive event then organised by Frost came in under budget.

Jack Frost Ball In the early days Frost always had a great deal of support from the distaff side. It was 1971 when we were celebrating ten years of Frost that it was decided to hold a Jack Frost Ball. The ladies of Frost took on the organisation. **Eileen Tye, Linda Gill** and other ladies put on a lavish function at Upper Court, a Georgian Manor on the Fairmile near Cobham, Surrey. Two hundred members, wives and guests in evening dress celebrated in grand fashion. An orchestra entertained, a banquet was served and **Roger Day** fell off the balcony. A tombola was held and provided much income for the event, particularly as Barbara, the lovely German friend of Gunter Schultz, managed not only to sell most tickets but she also sold the counterfoils. The Ball proved to be a most glorious one-off Frost event.

By the 80's we had moved our dinner venue to the **Dog and Fox in Wimbledon Village**. **Neil Durden-Smith** made a repeat guest appearance. Editor of Wisden Monthly, David Frith spoke here. It was in 1980 that much sought after speaker **Frank Crozier** made his first appearance, to be repeated in 1983 and yet again in 2000. Guests here included **Pat Pocock**. Through the good auspices of the then Chairman, Laurie Dillamore, in the 90's we held a series of dinners at the **Royal Automobile Club** in Pall Mall. This is a most impressive establishment and the more formal format proved most popular for Jack Frost XI members and their guests. Guest speakers here included sports guru, **John Bromley**, well known speaker **David Belchamber**; speaking at a Frost Dinner for the third time, and as a Jack Frost XI member, West Indian Test bowler; **Reg Scarlett**. In 1999 the club decided to endeavour to reduce the price of tickets and, obtaining a very good deal, the Annual Dinner was held with great success at **The Cricketer Club of London** in London's West End. The XI having, only a few weeks earlier, returned from the Tour of Australia a first class speech, reporting the tour, was delivered by Charles O'Reilly

Traditionally the front of the dinner menus have always shown a quotation made by or relating to a Froster over the previous year. The quote on the 1999 menu is typical. When an irate call from Heathrow Airport, where Jack Frost XI were about to board an aircraft to tour Australia, elicited a reply from David Dandridge "I could have sworn we departed tomorrow". The Presentation of Gnome of the Year, together with the accompanying Traffic Light is always part of the Jack Frost XI Dinner celebrations. The list of previous dinner speakers is printed on the back of the menu. Unfortunately, the turn out for the Annual Dinner has dropped to around the sixty mark. However the Jack Frost XI Annual Dinner is first class entertainment and remains the highlight of the close season.

Chapter IX – GNOMES AND OTHER LITTLE PEOPLE

In the early years of Jack Frost XI it became the custom for my to present an award to someone in the club who had done something of merit to benefit the club. There was no formal trophy just the requirement that they down a Traffic Light at the annual dinner. The original recipients are not recalled with the exception of Babs Clarke and the great and late Brian T.Buckle a lawyer of some eminence and favoured Froster. Things on the award front were about to change. In the early seventies Mr. Gill happened to be dancing at an hotel near Horsley when he bumped against a well set in the centre of the dance floor. Seated on the rim of the well was a smiling plaster gnome holding a fishing rod. **The Gnome of the Year** award was there and then born.

The first recipient had to be **C.W.M.Horner** who was born to be a gnome. Chris had been a loyal Froster since I had come across him playing for West End, Esher. He hailed from Blackhills, Esher and lived as he does now in Ladbroke Grove, the smart part. The following years it was natural that **Kim Morell** and **Sydney Smith** be awarded the Gnome for acts of buffoonery, but never to the standard of Horner. The original Gnomes soon formed a Gnomes dinner club which meet annually. The **Gnome Dinner** is still held today with the previous year's Gnome choosing the venue and organising the meal. Over the past three decades, Gnomes have met in many different places. **Robin Needham** took us to 'Miarnda's', a Soho strip club, **David Willis** to a prime Trust House hotel, **Brad Bradley** to the 'Players Theatre', **Peter Probyn** to the 'Swan Hotel', Pangbourne, **Michael Copleston** to his 'Kings Head' pub in Holmbury St. Mary. **Alistair Crowhurst** and **Nigel Fowler** took the Gnomes to 'School Dinners'. It is incumbent on the current holder of the Gnome that it be publicly displayed at all Jack Frost XI games and functions he is present.

The Gnome now presented is a second generation gnome. This came about following our match against Cricket Club of Geneva, held at the Oval. **Roger Hunt** was the Gnome at that time and duly placed the icon on the Oval turf by the players gate. In the general hullabaloo following this grand game the gnome was left behind. As Number One Gnome of Gnomes, Chris Horner, a few days later, went to recover the trophy. The Surrey Secretary advised Chris that it was probably still in the visitors changing room. England were playing West Indies that day when Chris presented himself at the Windies dressing room and enquired if anyone had seen a gnome. Looking behind him at an array of very tall lightning fast bowlers, the reply came 'There ain't no gnomes in here, Man' Chris set about replacing the lost icon. With the help of **Stephen Bartley**, bid at the Private Eye auction, in aid of their 'GoldenBalls Fund' to pay the costs of the libel action taken against them by Sir James Goldsmith. The gnome purchased was different in that it displayed prominent golden balls, making it less mantelpiece friendly than it's predecessor, as Peter Probyn's children will testify.

IX - GNOMES AND OTHER LITTLE PEOPLE

Whilst some may consider the Gnomes to be a club within a club, senior Gnome, Chris Horner puts it most clearly, 'The affairs of the Gnomes are the affairs of the Gnomes'.

Kennington Oval
Frosters and their Ladies enjoy lunch in a hospitality suite at the Oval in the nineties, organised by Chris Horner.

A Gnome
Wearing his Gnome tie, Brian Martin moves through the jeering diners to collect an award, at a R.A.C. Frost Dinner.

Frost Dinner
Long serving officer of the XI, Laurance Dillamore delivers an after dinner speech at the Royal Automobile Club, Pall Mall.

Chapter X - TO THE PRESENT

By the later 1970's there were perceptible changes in the management of Jack Frost XI. David Dandridge had become the driving force in his roll as joint Hon. Secretary, together with Bill Taylor, who with an active committee had continued to run things much in the same way as previously. A number of matches were tarted up by adding social events to the menu. Bill Taylor organised a most splendid meal in the Swan at Claygate, following the traditional October game with the Leverets at Hare Lane Green. During this time we were invited to take part in a charity match against **Vic Lewis's Showbusiness XI**, which was played at Blagdons, the Old Emmanuel ground. The match was much of a shambles and little to do with charity. Vic Lewis left a large bar bill which was settled by a generous Froster.

The big change came when Dandridge resigned and new Chairman and Secretary were elected at a meeting held at The Swan, Claygate. For the next two or three years Frost was effectively run by Neil Runkle, as Secretary, and Chairman John Watson a.k.a. Campbell. Without consultation with the membership this pair ran Jack Frost XI much as they wished. The crunch came when a delegation of leading Froster's approached The President, during a Test Match at Lord's, and spelt out that unless something was done, to remove the pair in charge, Jack Frost XI would flounder. A General Meeting was held, Watson and Runkle removed from office and a new committee elected with Brad Bradley as Chairman, Laurence Dillamore as Hon.Secretary and Charles O'Reilly became Hon. Treasurer. Later Laurence took over as Chairman. Long standing Frosters with the spirit of the club at heart had taken back the Jack Frost XI as we knew it. This committee reorganised the club management and not only put it on a sound financial footing but appointed match managers who would run games in the club's spirit.

One of the changes made concerned the Jack Frost XI Trust Fund. When the tourist returned from the 1975 Tour of California they brought back with them unused a four figure sum of sponsorship and other money. Over the following years sums were drawn from the fund to meet expenses for special matches against visiting overseas sides. British Columbia, Pasadena and **Toronto University** were amongst visitors from overseas who we entertained from the fund. The Trustees approval was sought and the new committee put it to a General Meeting, where it was approved, that the trust be broken and the balance transferred to a Special Account to fund Club Regalia. Charles O'Reilly put together a Jack Frost XI collection of City Ties, caps, sweaters and the like, funded from the Special Account. The small profit from the sale of the regalia to members would be paid back into the fund. This team ran the club with a great deal of success, for some ten years, until late in the 1990's when Dillamore and O'Reilly resigned and David Lipop took over the chairmanship with Alistair Crowhurst becoming Secretary and Peter Murray, Treasurer.

X - TO THE PRESENT

During the past twenty-five years many fixtures were added whilst retaining the best of the traditional list. One of the innovations included in the list some seasons was the President's Match. Games were held at **Esher, Teddington** and a private ground in Sunbury when the President raised an XI to play Jack Frost XI. These matches were held at the tail end of the season and the bulk of the players were invited from clubs Frost had played over that season. For a couple of years in the early nineties, Peter Murray organised a tour to the island of **Alderney** in the Channel Islands. Many Frosters flew out to enjoy the cricket and socialising. On one occasion there was some speculation that Ian Botham, who had a home on the island, may play for Frost. The President, on learning of this possibility, sent an instruction to the Tour Manager that this must not happen. Playing our fixture against **Broadhalfpenny Brigands at Hambledon,** the 'Cradle of Cricket' is a feather in the Frost cap, as few new fixtures are taken on at this historic venue.

Whilst the ground is owned by Winchester College and leased by the Royal Navy it provides cricket for local cricketers playing under the Brigands banner. The view over many surrounding counties is quite breathtaking all though, on a dull day, a harsh wind cuts the players in half. Broad-Halfpenny Down is overlooked by the famous Bat and Ball Inn, where the memorabilia and ghosts of John Nyren and William Beldham haunt back to the eighteenth century. From the turn of the 21st century the Cricket Club will have a rebuilt pavilion. Across the border in Surrey, the fixture against nearby **Tilford**, is played on a delightful village green, which was chosen for the location of the television version of the cricket match immortalised in A.G.MacDonell's famous novel **'England, Their England'**. Chris Wilson has managed this match since the first game. The **Charterhouse XI** fixture is on the playing field of the famous school where P.B.H.May made his first runs. This game is run by Robin Cheeseman on a Sunday in May.

Adding to the clubs we have over the years played in Bushy Park, is **National Physical Laboratory** a most recent and popular fixture. A rare London fixture for Jack Frost XI is **Putney Cricket Club**, played on the Heath where we have already built strong rapport. **Abinger**, is a most delightful village ground on a slope towards a stream. Adjacent to the main Guildford to Dorking road, this match is played around the time of the August Bank Holiday. Simon Klimcke, in 1999, organised Jack Frost XI drawn, in the main, from members who had, the previous winter, toured Australia.

Larger and Chips in the Sun Towards the end of the 90's a tour, under the direction of Brian Martin, was organised to the Costa Blanca, Spain. Two games were played against **Javea Cricket Club** who played on matting surrounded by very uneven scrubland. The weather was diabolical with storms bringing downpours of rain that blocked the drains and roads.

X – TO THE PRESENT

A large and mixed party of Frosters flew from Gatwick Airport and stayed in an apartment block in Javea which lacked catering and a bar. However, local bars and cafes provided lager and the local Mediterranean food of hamburgers, hot dogs and fish in batter all accompanied by chips. Apart from one particularly objectionable pushy Spaniard, the opposition were made up of expatriate English all bedecked with gold chains, medallions, rings and earrings, and they were the men.

Luncheon in a St. John's Wood Garden Shed In the early nineties, Laurence Dillamore and Charles O'Reilly used some influence to obtain, for a number of years, an **'Arbour' for the Lord's Test,** for the use of Jack Frost XI. A party of thirty or some members met at each Test Match in a ground-mower shed on the edge of the Nursery Ground to devour table loads of food and great quantities of wine, beer and spirits. Seats in the Compton & Edrich stand were provided for Frosters. Splendid days were enjoyed, with many friends and opponents visiting the **Jack Frost XI Arbour.**

When this part of the Lord's ground was scheduled for re-development Chris Horner arranged a luncheon in a hospitality suite at the **Oval** to watch the Australians play Surrey, where some two dozen members watched cricket and enjoyed lunch.

AUSTRALIA - "COMISSATORES NEQUE PILARI"

During the season of 1998 Jack Frost XI were, with only the exception of Teddington C.C., unbeaten on the field of play. It was therefore with a light step that on 28th December 1998 a party of some thirty Frosters; less 'Dorothy' who thought the tour left the following day, their ladies and friends, embarked by air for Sydney, Australia to play seven games of cricket, in and around Sydney. This tour should be seen in the context that very few long established cricket clubs have managed an Australian Tour. Therefore a wandering club such as Jack Frost XI broke much new ground.

In 1996 the tour had been proposed by Mr.Gill and Laurence Dillamore to celebrate the fortieth birthday of the club. However, it was decided to coincide the tour with England's visit to **Australia** over the 1998/9 winter. In the event both Gill and Dillamore were unable to tour thus management fell into the hands of William Lewis and local Jack Frost XI member, Garth Jones who is resident in Manly, New South Wales. Jack Frost XI were soon in action against **Manly Warratahs** at Knolans, Sydney on New Year's Eve. Overtaking the Warratahs total of 161 (Norman Gray 3 for 33) Frost won with four wickets in hand after Tim Klimcke and Mike Chase both scored unbeaten half centuries. Thus Frost chalked up a win in the Southern hemisphere during 1998. A match of note was played against the **Cricketers Club of New South Wales.** Charles O'Reilly's, 90 not out to take Frost to 171 proved insufficient. However MCC led by Roger Knight, playing the same club on an adjacent wicket, fared less well. The evening proved a greater success when the two

X - TO THE PRESENT

visiting clubs were hosted to a splendid dinner by the **Cricketers Club of New South Wales**. In the speeches stakes our captain, Mike Chase, out performed the secretary of MCC, Roger Knight.

The highlight of the tour was the game at **The Bradman Oval, Bowral**. Jack Frost XI were honoured to be granted a game at Australia's most prestigious venue, where there are 800 application per year for games on the Bowral Ground. In all Jack Frost XI won three of their seven games, all of which were played on a limited overs basis. This was not a bad result as Jack Frost XI had never, in its then 39 year history, played this genre of the game. Charles O'Reilly led the tour batting making 171 runs in 4 innings with an average of 85.5. He was closely followed by Tim Klimcke, Mike Chase and Rohan Leek. The leading bowlers were Simon Klimcke; 7 wickets at an average of 13.6, Stuart Stennett 10 wickets, Alistair Crowhurst 5 wickets and Norman Gray 7 wickets. The **Australian Cricket Team** visited the tour hotel, Steyne Hotel, Manly, where David Dandridge introduced Steve Waugh, Shane Warne and McGrath before huddling down to discuss finer points of the game.

Jack Frost XI showed it's hospitality, hosting an evening booze-up and feed, for opponents on a boat around Sydney Harbour. Whilst Bill Lewis led the tour party, much of the detail and match arrangements were made by Garth Jones who in the past has brought over the Manly Warratahs to play Frost in England.

Jack Frost XI in Australia 1999
The club played at Victoria Barracks, New South Wales, on this tour. The very smart Jack Frost XI team photographed, shows XIII players.

Chapter XI – WHAT'S IT ALL ABOUT?

So for the past forty season the Founder and President has enjoyed much Jack Frost XI cricket, as recounted in these pages. More importantly Tony Gill has made literally hundreds of friends over the past four decades. Not only friends within Jack Frost XI itself but also due to the cricket the club has played. Mr. Gill sincerely hopes that all Frosters will get the same pleasure from their playing Jack Frost XI cricket. From early beginnings the child was born and thence flourished because so many sportsmen enjoyed playing the Frost brand of cricket. Many of the players of yesteryear have encouraged and introduced their sons to play Frost cricket. Now many have retired from playing and are still supporting the club in a number of different ways. What the future holds no one person knows, so much depending on the development of the game internationally.

The Jack Frost XI President does however wish that in the future the principles originally laid down and followed to the present will continue. I wish that rather than see Jack Frost XI play Leverets on the Internet the game is played on the surface of the Moon. The President apologises in advance for his absence as he is sure that he will not be up to the lunar travelling. I have much enjoyed writing this account of a wandering club, which I achieved, over three months, totally from memory. This only goes to show how devoted I am to Jack Frost XI cricket. This account of Jack Frost XI cricket over the past forty years is entitled 'The Early Years' in the hope and trust that there will be many more happy Frosting years to come.

Tony Gill, Founder and President – Jack Frost XI 10th March 2000

Marin County, Fairfax, Northern California
On Sunday 6th April, 1975 Frost played Marin C.C. on the beautiful White Hill School ground, across the Golden Gate Bridge.

P.J.
Peter Probyn, a Froster from way back in the 70's was the leading light in 'F' Troop and played most of his cricket at Bristol Optimists. On one occasion, during a Frost Game on the College Close, Tony Gill bowled two consecutive maiden overs to David Gravney, then with Gloucestershire C.C.C., now Chairman of England Selectors. Afterwards Gravel went on record saying "Tony Gill was the most dangerous bowler he had ever faced". There was a hush on the close that night.

The Senior Professionals in Javea
Brad Bradley and Chris Horner pose for a Coca-Cola advertisement.

APPENDIX I

When in 1990, the Leveret Cricket Club ceased to play cricket on Hare Lane Green, Jack Frost XI were their final fixture, after thirty games between the two clubs. On 6th October, 1990, Tony Gill wrote and performed his Requiem in The Swan, Claygate, as follows:-

REQUIEM TO A YOUNG HARE
Prancing, dancing with playful skip
through two great wars with nare a slip.
Riparian green, mere postage stamp
play oft shadowed by bright street lamp.

Bounded by busy lane called hare.
Only now did cease play so fair.
River Rythe may give deep sigh
to our young friends we say "Goodbye".

Red hares, they can go grey,
sometimes they even fade away.
But let us not rue the day.
Whilst nearby Swan did bray
as old and young, like hares, did play.

Nineteen centuries and sixty one
October Jack Frost join the fun.
Cavorting on the green as one
a long marriage had begun.

The frosty bowlers bore the brunt
and were never in the hunt.
By ten wickets they did lose
before commencing on the booze.

Thirty years they oned and foured
on green sward, with added mat
Sometimes with ball and oft with bat.
Frost and hare never to forget
many long years of Leveret.

Anthony 6th October 1990
c 1990 The Bard - Tony Gill as published in the 'Daily Telegraph'

Jack Frost XI and Humphrey
The XI at the Royal Household in the 1980's, together with Stephen Bartley's famous dog.

Frost in Spain
William Lewis appears to be concerned about David Lipop's height.

Appendix II – EARLIER HISTORY

Since completing the writing of the main body of this work, The Early Years - Jack Frost XI 1961 - 1999, which I would remind you has been compiled by memory, I have received (from Mike Copleston) a copy of the wonderful publication, put together by then Club Historian, **Richard Greenwood, Jack Frost XI - History and Statistics 1961 -1970.**

Reading through this work I find far more detail, and a different objective view of the earliest year brought about Greenwood's own involvement and access to the club records, up to 1970. I consider it important to put on the record by including extracts from this earlier work.

In this appendix, I record both extracts and my great thanks to Richard Greenwood, a very loyal Froster, for his earlier record of Jack Frost XI.

SELECTED EXTRACTS FROM RICHARD GREENWOOD'S "HISTORY AND STATISTICS". COMPILED IN 1970.

"If the statistics are published, why not," they asked, "the history of the XI?" The fact that the XI had existed for only ten years daunted none but the person given the task of compiling the information.

Perhaps in the future, volumes of tales of Jack Frost 'happenings' will be produced. Those stories have been omitted here in the hope that the History will appeal to non members and qualified members alike.
(Author's italics)

The Origin

There were no comets seen; no gory happenings; apparently little to attract the interest of the augurs. But perhaps they could 'read' H.C.A.Gill as well as he could 'read' the wrong 'un, for there was evidence enough that something was about to happen on the cricket scene.

When, on **8th October, 1961,** the Leveret Cricket Club found themselves at the last moment without an end-of-season fixtures, one of their members, Tony Gill raised an XI, called it, in deference to the time of the year, **Jack Frost XI** and issued a challenge. Unwittingly had begun a club that was to give pleasure over the ensuing ten years to many participants and supporters of the game. Little can be said of the match:- Jack Frost batted first and after the fall of the 4th wicket with the score at 70, the remaining wickets added but fifteen runs between them. In reply, the Leverets romped home without the loss of a wicket. Jack Frost have now played ten matches on the beguiling Leveret ground where cover, umpire and deep square leg are equidistant from the bat and where, in their innocence, lesser mortals scoff at the failings of greater men who

Appendix II – EARLIER HISTORY

are beckoned, Siren-like, to their downfall on the boundary. It is certainly one of the most sociable of fixtures and the evenings in the 'Swan' are memorable.

That the XI lost the match by 10 wickets (due it has been remarked, to the presence of eleven captains in the side) deterred neither the Leverets, who offered Jack Frost the fixture the following year,nor the 'visiting' captain, who swore revenge. Thus it was that the XI was launched, though it was to be some time before the club was formally constituted.

RAISON D'ETRE

Though referred to as a club, it has not at this stage been officially constituted and it was still in reality Tony Gill's XI. It was generally agreed that the object of the XI should be to extend the season at both ends.......The object of the XI was noticed by the 'Esher News' several years later when, writing a preview of local clubs in April 1969, their reporter accurately observed: *'Although, inevitably, the Jack Frost XI have started already and will probably go on longer than anyone else, cricket does not officially get under way until this weekend.'*
Author's italics

The 1963 season began in April with an excellent match against the Old Citizens. With nearly 300 runs scored in an exciting match in April, who could fail to appreciate the objects of XI? Evidently the Old Citizens approved: several of their side later played for Jack Frost and became qualified members, and K.I.Morell was elected Chairman in 1966.

Jack Frost XI v Old Citizens 28th April 1963
OLD CITIZENS

R.Thatcher b Woodbury	1
P.Busby lbw b Woodbury	10
P.Sawell ct. Coops b Herman	12
I.Brown not out	100
K.I.Morell b Miller	22
G.Smith ct. Jones b Hawtin	12
C.Crawford ct. Bright b Woodbury	6
C.Dicker not out	1
Extras:	8
(6 wkts.dec.)	172

Did not bat G.Sachs, R.Brown, M.Roots

Appendix II - EARLIER HISTORY

JACK FROST XI

J.Tyler ct. Busby b Brown	49
A.J.Miller b Roots	4
R.Hunt ct. Busby b Smith	66
L.Coops b Sawell	9
O.W.Herman b Roots	36
D.Davy not out	1
D.Jones not out	4
Extras:	2
5 wkts.)	171

Did not bat: A.J.Hawtin, B.Bright, C.T.Woodbury, H.C.A.Gill.

Result: Match Drawn

Author's Note: O.W.Herman, known as 'Lofty', opened the bowling for Hampshire between the Wars and became a First-Class Umpire after W.W.II

– ooOoo –

The Inaugural Meeting of Jack Frost XI was held on 30th November 1964. Six players were present and it was then that the Constitution and Rules of the Club were adopted, Officers elected and a subscription of 10/6d. for "Qualified" members (after a playing qualification of three games) approved.

– ooOoo –

TOURS

The following extract, taken from the 'Ringwood and Fordingbridge Journal' of 22nd June 1966 captures the essential approach of Frost on tour:

'Touring Cricketers At Ringwood'
When that intrepid crowd of cricketing enthusiasts under the banner of "Jack Frost" converged upon Ringwood and opened their innings in the bar of the 'Smith's Arms' on Wednesday, they were bent on making this tour of the New Forest a smashing success and a smashing success it has been.'

Appendix II – EARLIER HISTORY

Led by Tony Gill, who founded the Jack Frost XI about five years ago, these players, drawn in the main from well known London clubs, are dedicated to the game for the game's sake, filling in the gap between the end of one season and the beginning of the next, with a fixture list which carries on right through the winter and spring.

The whole team agrees that their leadership is inspired by almost fanatical fervour, and their ability to snatch defeat in the moment of victory is unique in the annals of the game.

FULL DAY

On Friday they rounded off a full day with a dinner at the 'Crown Hotel', Ringwood, sitting down with their opponents of the afternoon, the "Gentlemen of All Hampshire".

With four matches, a golf tournament, a gala dinner and a farewell champagne party behind them, as they concluded this tour they can compliment themselves upon nobly upholding the fair name of cricket both on the field and off.'

– ooOoo –

Though it is yet the intention of the XI to continue to enjoy tours in these islands, the advent of cheap air flights has encouraged talk of a short tour to Portugal; indeed, there is rumour of a trip to the U.S.A. in 1973!

Author's Note: Portugal did not happen, but the tour to the U.S.A. took place in 1975.

– ooOoo –

Playing more games inevitably meant that there were more qualified members so that by the end of 1965 the number had reached 46.

The years 1965-1967 were years of consolidation. Membership increased steadily and, with regular fixtures against Burnham in their cricket week and matches against, Pyrford, Rudgwick, Wibbandune and Westcot, as well as some strong fixtures on tour, the XI was beginning to settle to a wide range of fixtures.

– ooOoo –

Appendix II – EARLIER HISTORY

BOXING DAY
It was during this period, in 1966, that the XI played the first of the 20 overs-a-side Boxing Day matches at Teddington and, since 1969, at Surbiton. Of the five fixtures arranged, only one has been cancelled due to poor conditions.

Author's Note: Apart from the 1999 tour to Australia, Jack Frost XI have always refused to participate in limited over games except for special games, completely out of season.

From the 'Esher News', 30th December, 1966
"Twenty two brave men left their cold turkey and wine on Boxing Day to pull on their flannels, shirts and jerseys and play cricket. The only hint of winter was that the players wore football boots, for the game was played in bright sunshine.
The players came from Jack Frost XI and Teddington, and the match was played at Bushy Park, Teddington's home ground. The hosts won the match by 20 runs. This was the first Boxing Day match between the two sides, although talk of the fixture has been going on for some seasons.
  To consider the problem of the obviously heavy ground, the match was played on a matted wicket. Football boots were worn as the outfield was, in places, muddy.
  The teams were extremely fortunate, for the weather was kind, bright sunshine providing favourable conditions and, of course, good light.
  The game was limited to twenty overs a side, with lunch between innings. The match started at 11.45.a.m.
  Teddington batted first and soon lost a wicket to B.Lay, but some middle order play saw their total reach 123. R.Greenwood and R.Hunt were the most successful bowlers, taking two wickets each.
  Jack Frost XI also lost quick wickets, but K.Morell, with an innings of 34, pulled them nearer the winning score. The tail, however, could not keep up the quick scoring rate and by the end of the twenty overs the side had managed 103 for 8 - still twenty runs behind"
  Groundsmen have always been satisfied with the condition of hallowed turf at the end of the contest. Indeed, after the match in 1969, the 'Times', reporting the London Hockey League match at Surbiton, stated 'The Surbiton pitch, as ever, was in perfect condition for all the 500 runs that had been scored on it on Boxing Day.'
  Following some correspondence in the 'Daily Telegraph' in 1969 and H.Sidney Smith's reply, '... In the first weekend of October they (i.e. Jack Frost XI) has one match in Claygate, in Surrey, and two sides were in the autumn sunshine on the Sunday. The final fixture for 1969 is on December 26th at Teddington...' considerable interest was shown in the XI. 'I was thrilled to read in the 'Daily Telegraph' that there

Appendix II – EARLIER HISTORY

is even a remote prospect of seeing any cricket at all in England during the winter.', was just one example of the enthusiastic replies. There is certainly never any difficulty in the raising of a side.

BENEFIT MATCHES

A MIDDLESEX XII
H.Latchman l.b.w. b Scott		14
T.Selwood ct.Sawyer b Needham		45
J.Black ct.Dandridge b Needham		32
P.Parfitt b Danford		46
K.Barrington Not Out		51
W.E.Russell ct.Stephenson b Danford		1
F.Stuart Not Out		1
Extras:		3
(5 wkts. dec.)		193

Did not bat: K.Jones, M.Smith, C.T.Radley, N.Featherstone, M.Rowlatt.

JACK FROST XI
A.R.Hunt ct.Black b Barrington		43
D.P.Dandridge ct.Featherstone b Rowlatt		12
P.Sawyer ct. & b Barrington		25
J.Scott ct.Latchman b Barrington		17
M.Copleston Not Out		11
M.Danford ct.Latchman b Rowlatt		15
Extras:		4
(5 wkts.)		127

Did not bat: P.Needham, R.A.Furness, P.Stevenson, A.Gill, D.Carmichael

Appendix II - EARLIER HISTORY

RECENT DEVELOPMENT
Author's Note: 1970, of course.
The Captain's burden was considerably eased in 1968 with the introduction of the Match Manager system, and the following year the rules were amended so that qualification for playing membership became three games in any one year followed by two games in each of the succeeding three years.

The last two years (1969-1970) have seen a strengthening of the fixture list with matches against Twickenham, Teddington, Reigate Priory, Byfleet, Oxshott and Little Kingshill. The number of matches played in 1970 rose to 31, qualified membership to 108, and by the end of the season, 65 different clubs had been played in the first ten years.

THE FUTURE
What is the future of the XI to be? The Club has come a long way in a short time. It maintains the original object of extending the season at both ends, at the same time catering for a wide range of ability. Members remain primarily members of another club but play for the XI when it is their wish. Certainly various changes must come, especially where the burden of management rests too heavily on too few shoulders. The number of games will probably be extended so that by 1973 the XI will be able to offer a match on every Sunday throughout the season.

Frost thrives. In an age when we read so much of the poor spirit in which the game is played, perhaps we are fortunate that we have not lost sight of what the king of sports is all about.

"For cricket in sooth is Sovran King of sport" Authors Note: So wrote Richard Greenwood in 1970. I believe his words are just as relevant in the year 2000.

Appendix II – EARLIER HISTORY

LONG SERVING MEMBERS

Listed below are twenty-eight, present day, members of Jack Frost XI who played for the Club in the first ten years (1961-1970). Several of these are thankfully still playing for the Club.

	Date of FIRST MATCH	Date QUALIFIED
O.A.(Brad) Bradley	6.20.68	19.6.69
M.Citroen	21.6.67	29.6.68
M.V.G.Copleston	20.6.67	4.7.67
R.Crawford	27.4.68	14.8.68
D.P.Dandridge	17.8.67	8.10.67
R.H.Davey	16.7.67	13.4.69
A.Denning	2.10.6	18.6.65
L.Dillamore	27.4.68	23.6.68
H.C.A.Gill	8.10.61	7.10.63
R.M.Gill	16.6.63	6.9.64
N.Gray	18.6.70	11.8.70
R.G.Greenwood	23.9.62	12.10.63
J.A.Hawtin	8.10.61	7.10.63
C.W.M.Horner	19.9.64	25.4.65
A.R.Hunt	23.9.6	22.9.63
P.King	1.10.67	27.4.68
B.H.Martin	19.6.68	6.10.68
K.I.Morell	7.10.62	23.9.63
P.Needham	20.8.69	15.6.70
B.Rhodes	5.6.66	29.4.67
P.Skerett	20.6.64	8.9.68
R.Thatcher	17.6.65	19.6.65
L.Tye	14.8.68	18.6.69
M.P.R.Welch	4.9.66	10.9.67
R.White	8.9.68	24.7.69
D.Willis	21.8.66	1.10.66
E.Wilson	25.5.70	19.6.70

T.J.Booth has been an Honorary Member since 1970

LONG STANDING FIXTURES

Jack Frost XI have been playing five clubs for over thirty years.

Ockham	first played on 16th May, 1965
Thursley	3rd October 1965
Rudgwick	25th September 1966
Teddington	20th August 1969
Oxshott	10th June 1970

Appendix II – EARLIER HISTORY

Javea Cricket Ground - Spain
As David Lipop walks in, Simon Klimcke walks out during a match against Javea Cricket Club, mainly drawn from English expatriates.

Javea Cricket Club Pavilion
There was much lounging in the sun, and hiding from the rain, during the Jack Frost XI Tour to Spain in the mid-90's.

Appendix II – EARLIER HISTORY

STATISTICAL JOTTING

Over the years there have been many playing achievements, to many to recount in full. However, here are a few figures, of some interest, from the first ten years of Jack Frost XI
The following player has carried his bat:
A.J.Miller 45* v Bootleggers 13.6.65
The following openers batted for the duration of the innings:
R.Hunt: 108* v Wibbandune 5.10.69
B.Martin: 63* v Wimborne 20.6.69
H.C.A.Gill liked bowling at Westcott. In 1967 he took 2 wickets in a 4 ball spell, but managed to give away 5 runs. Two years later in an eight ball spell he took 3 wickets without conceding a run.
Between 1961 and 1970 A.Gill took 20 catches, A.Hawtin 18, M.Copleston 15, K.Morell 15, R.Greenwood 14, R.Hunt 11 and C.Horner 9, whilst D.Dandridge took 7.
Only Brian Moreton (100* in 138 mins.) v Wibbandune (6.10.68) scored a century in their debut for the club.

Brian Rhodes took 7 for 27 in 11 overs against Pyrford (5.6.66) in his debut for the club.
In a low scoring match at Graffham, the home side was bowled out for 50 (Hawtin 6-26, Greenwood 4-24). The highest score for Jack Frost XI was by M.Welch, 8* and the XI were defeated by 23 runs.
In the match against Sons of Bacchus in 1969 the opposition employed 9 bowlers, seven of whom were used against the opening pair, Richard Davey and Kim Morell.
In a match, written up in the Daily Mirror, against Ancient Mariners, at Hambledon in Surrey, Michael Copleston scored 105 not out then took the first eight wickets, caught the 9th and bowled the 10th, finishing with 9 for 17. With his score on 99 the umpire, Laurence Dillamore, had turned down an appeal for caught behind.

AUTHORS NOTE

This appendix goes a long way towards dotting the I's and crossing the T's of the history of Jack Frost XI. The authors thanks go out to Richard Greenwood for compiling the original document and to Michael Copleston for coming up with his well thumbed copy.